30 minute
indian

30 minute
indian

Cook modern
Indian recipes in
30 minutes or less.

Sunil Vijayakar

Photography by William Reavell

LAUREL
GLEN

First published in North America in 2000 by
Laurel Glen Publishing
An imprint of the Advantage Publishers Group
5880 Oberlin Drive, San Diego, CA 92121-4794
www.advantagebooksonline.com

ISBN   1-57145-672-4 (hardcover)
       1-57145-678-3 (paperback)

Library of Congress Cataloging-in-Publication Data available upon
request.

Printed in China.

1 2 3 4 5   00 01 02 03 04

Notes

1 Standard level spoon measurements are used in all recipes.
2 Eggs should be medium unless otherwise stated. The USDA advises
   that eggs should not be consumed raw. This book contains dishes
   made with raw or lightly cooked eggs. It is prudent for more
   vulnerable people, such as pregnant and nursing mothers, invalids,
   the elderly, babies, and young children, to avoid uncooked or lightly
   cooked dishes made with eggs. Once prepared, these dishes should
   be kept refrigerated and used promptly.
3 Milk should be whole unless otherwise stated.
4 Fresh herbs should be used unless otherwise stated. If unavailable,
   use dried herbs as an alternative, but halve the quantities stated.
5 Pepper should be freshly ground black pepper unless otherwise
   stated.
6 Ovens should be preheated to the specified temperature—if using a
   convection oven, follow the manufacturer's instructions for adjusting
   the time and the temperature.
7 This book includes dishes made with nuts and nut derivatives. It is
   advisable for customers with known allergic reactions to nuts and
   nut derivatives and those who may be potentially vulnerable to these
   allergies, such as pregnant and nursing mothers, invalids, the elderly,
   babies, and children, to avoid dishes made with nuts and nut oils. It
   is also prudent to check the labels of preprepared ingredients for the
   possible inclusion of nut derivatives.
8 Vegetarians should look for special labeling on cheese to ensure that
   it is made with vegetarian rennet. There are vegetarian forms of
   Parmesan, feta, cheddar, Cheshire, Red Leicester, dolcelatte, and many
   goat cheeses, among others.

Executive Editor: Polly Manguel
Project Editor: Cara Frost
Copy-editor: Linda Doeser
Creative Director: Keith Martin
Senior Designer: David Godfrey
Production Controller: Lisa Moore
Photographer: William Reavell
Stylist: Liz Hippisley
Home Economist: Sunil Vijayakar

North American Edition
Managing Editor: JoAnn Padgett
Project Editor: Elizabeth McNulty

contents

introduction

I think my love of food stems from the Sunday mornings I spent with my father as a young boy, growing up in Bombay. A film director with a hectic work and social life, he would make Sunday the day when he would stop and cook a big lunch for a large group of family and friends. He would pile me into his Morris Minor and off we would head for the bustling bazaars and markets. Armed with shopping bags, we would wander through endless aisles of vegetable and fruit stalls, then into open courtyards full of fresh fish and shellfish, piled onto blocks of ice, and into tiny little stalls with colorful pyramids of spices, nuts, and dried fruits.

This was an experience which assailed all the senses, the visual feast of wicker baskets piled high with bright green bunches of coriander, mint, and fenugreek. Wooden crates of mangoes, papayas, and ruby-red pomegranates, mountains of fresh ginger, onions, and garlic. The tactile experience of touching and tasting the produce, the aromas of all the dried spices, and above all, the cacophony of the market sellers plying their wares. Laden with our shopping, we would wend our way home and into the kitchen, where dad would effortlessly conjure up a veritable feast, all the time talking with great passion about different foods and ingredients and making me his official taster. He instilled in me a love and passion for food, with his relaxed attitude to preparation and cooking and most importantly the gift and joy of sharing food.

In this book and through these recipes, I hope I can share with you some of the recipes I have enjoyed and continue to enjoy cooking on a frequent basis. The frenetic pace of our modern life often limits the time we have to spend preparing, cooking, and experimenting with food. These recipes are all quick and easy to prepare and will give you a taste of Indian cuisine, which you can easily incorporate into your cooking on a daily basis.

A well-stocked pantry of basic ingredients and spices is essential. Most of these can be bought in large supermarkets, but I would urge you to go to an Indian or Asian market and stock up on a range of ingredients for your pantry. All spices, whole or ground, should be stored in airtight containers, in a cool, dark place. Some of the recipes call for a long list of spices and other ingredients; do not let this intimidate you. Just make sure that you have everything laid out and on hand before you start to cook, and the rest will be easy. You will realize that cooking Indian food is like painting a picture; if you have an organized palette to work with, you can create anything you desire.

The main ingredients for cooking wonderful food are not, however, to be found in spice jars, supermarkets, or bazaars, but in the passion, love, and joy of cooking, eating, and sharing food. Armed with this, you cannot go wrong.

glossary

Amchur
Raw green mango powder, pale yellow in color. Used in dishes to add tartness with a hint of sweetness. If unavailable, substitute ½ teaspoon of lemon or lime juice for 1 teaspoon of amchur.

Asafoetida
A resin from the plant, it is extremely strong in flavor and aroma and is used only in tiny quantities. It is available in small plastic boxes and should be stored tightly closed. As well as flavor, asafoetida has great digestive powers.

Atta or Chapatti Flour
This medium-grade flour is used to make most Indian unleavened breads. This may be bought at any Indian grocers. Ordinary wholemeal flour may also be used for Indian breads, very well sieved.

Basmati Rice
This distinctive long grain rice is very popular as an accompaniment to meat and vegetable dishes.

Cardamom
Little green pods with tiny black-brown seeds, very aromatic in flavor. They come in three varieties: green, white and black. The green and white pods can be used for both sweet and savory dishes or to flavor rice, the black only for savory dishes. The pods are used whole in rice dishes or the seeds are lightly crushed or ground and used to flavor sweets and other dishes. It is one of the main components of garam masala.

Cashew Nuts
Grown on the western coast of India, these nuts are used in curries, rice dishes and desserts. They are usually roasted or fried before being used.

Cassia
Also known as 'Chinese cinnamon', this bark is stronger in flavor than cinnamon and has a slightly thicker texture. It can easily be substituted with cinnamon, if unavailable.

Chilies, dried
These red chilies are used to flavor dishes, usually by frying them in hot oil. There are a few varieties such as the Kashmiri and Round chilies. Chili flakes are also used in cooking to give a fiery 'heat' to food. Use with caution.

Chilies, fresh green and red
The chilies used in Indian food are usually the long green, slender variety and can be very hot in flavor. To lessen the heat of a chili, when using, carefully remove the seeds by splitting the chili in half lengthways, using gloves if need be. Fresh red chilies are simply ripened green chilies and have the same intensity of heat.

Chili Powder
Mild, medium and hot chili powders are made from powdered dried chilies. If using for the first time, experiment with the amount that you use.

Cinnamon
Cinnamon is the thinly rolled inner bark of an evergreen tree that grows mainly in southern India and Sri Lanka, in Madagascar and in the West Indies. Used in stick or powdered form, this bark is used to flavor rice dishes, curries and sweets. It can be substituted with cassia bark if the recipe calls for it.

Cloves
This very strongly-flavored and aromatic spice is used in many curry and rice dishes. Ground or powdered cloves are used in very small quantities because of their pungency. It is also sometimes used to seal a betel leaf for serving after an Indian meal.

Coconut
Fresh coconut flesh is widely used in many Indian dishes, grated or ground to a paste. To obtain the flesh from a coconut, the easiest way I have found is to put it into a thick plastic bag and slam it hard on a concrete floor. There will be some water in it which you can save and then you should prise the flesh from the tough outer shell with a sharp knife. Once this is done, remove the thin brown skin, using a vegetable peeler. To get grated coconut for a recipe, cut the flesh into small pieces and process in a food processor or blender, until you get tiny flakes. You can also use a conventional grater, which is time consuming, but you will get a smoother texture. Grated coconut freezes well if stored in an airtight freezer bag and is always useful to have on hand.

Coconut Milk
Providing texture and flavor to meat and vegetable dishes, this milk is widely available in supermarkets and is sold in 13 oz cans.

Coriander
This spice is sold as whole seeds, which are light brown and round, or

as a ground powder. It is an essential spice in Indian cooking.

Cilantro
This fragrant and aromatic herb is widely used in Indian cuisine and is an important ingredient for many dishes, chutneys and salads.

Cumin
These little brown grain-like seeds are used whole, fried or roasted, in Indian dishes. In its ground form, cumin is an essential base to many dishes, from curries to rice.

Curry Leaves
These leaves are small and dark green and are often sold fresh in Indian greengrocers. They are usually fried before use, to impart an aromatic flavor to any dish or pickle.

Dhal
These are beans and lentils and there are over sixty different types. The better known are listed below, and are available in Indian grocery stores and large supermarkets. Masoor dhal are split, skinless, red lentils. They are dark brown when whole but when split and the skin is removed , the colour is bright pinky orange.
Moong dhal are split, skinless, moong lentils. They are dark green when whole but once split and skinned they are yellow and oval shaped.
Channa dhal are split, black, gram lentils, They are from the chick-pea family but are smaller and have a dark brown husk. When split and skinned they are bright yellow and resemble yellow split peas. Gram flour (besan) is made from these lentils.

Dhana-jeera
A mixture of powdered coriander and cumin seeds, sold in Asian greengrocers. You can make your own mix by grinding together 1 teaspoon of cumin seeds and 2 teaspoons coriander seeds.

Fennel Seeds
These light green seeds have a flavor of anise and are slightly bigger than cumin seeds. They are also eaten, lightly roasted, after an Indian meal as a digestive.

Fenugreek Seeds and Leaves
These tiny, pebble-like, mustard-yellow seeds have an earthy flavor and are mainly used in pickles and vegetarian cooking. When the seeds are sprouted, it results in a spinach-like leaf, which is used to flavor breads and other dishes.

Garam Masala
This is a ground spice mix, used to flavor food. It can be bought in ready-made commercial jars or packets. However, there is nothing like making your own, as it will have much more pungency and flavor. The main ingredients are cardamom, cinnamon or cassia bark, cloves and black peppercorns. Here is a recipe for making you own. Once made, store in an airtight jar and use when required.

1 tablespoon cassia or cinnamon
   sticks, broken up
1 tablespoon cardamom pods
1 teaspoon whole cloves
3 teaspoons cumin seeds
2 teaspoons black peppercorns

In a dry, hot frying pan, roast the spices for 1–2 minutes, or until you can smell the aroma. Cool and place in a coffee grinder and blend until you have a fine powder. Store in an airtight jar. This mixture will keep for 3–4 months.

Garlic
Indispensable to most Indian cooking, fresh garlic is used peeled and finely crushed, chopped or sliced. A quick way to get crushed garlic is to use a fine grater.

Ginger
This rhizome is an integral part of most Indian cooking, along with garlic and onions (the essential base of most Indian food). Make sure you get fresh ginger which has a smooth light brown skin. To use, peel and either slice into slivers or fine dice, or finely grate, saving and using any juice.

Gram Flour
A fine, pale yellow colored flour made from chickpeas. It is used in many recipes from breads to vegetable curries.

Green Mangoes
The unripe fruit with green skin is used mainly as a pickle ingredient and sometimes to add a tangy flavor to curries.

Jaggery
Raw cane sugar, sold in blocks or molds and widely used to sweeten or balance any hot, spicy dish. However,if not available, soft brown cane sugar can easily replace it.

Mango Pulp
A versatile ingredient, usually used to flavor drinks.

glossary

Mustard Seeds
Brown and black mustard seeds are used as an essential part of flavoring in Indian cooking. They are usually fried quickly in hot oil until they start to pop and they flavor many pickles, vegetarian dishes, dhals and rice dishes. They have a wonderfully nutty flavor when cooked.

Nigella
Also known as black onion seeds, these tiny tear-drop seeds are very aromatic when cooked and are used to flavor breads and pickles.

Nutmeg
Nutmeg is the seed of the nutmeg tree. It grows within a lacy cage of mace, inside a fleshy peach-like fruit. It is dried in the sun after havesting, and is sold both whole and in powdered form. Although very hard to grate, the whole nutmeg may be cracked easily with a hammer. It is best bought whole as the ground form soon loses its fragrance.

Okra
Known as bhindi in India, okra are the seed pods of a member of the hibiscus family. Choose bright green, firm specimens with no signs of browning

Onion Seeds
Black in color and triangular in shape, these are used for both pickles and vegetable curries.

Paan
Betel leaf dressed with calcium paste, fennel seeds wrapped and held together with a clove and sometimes covered with varq, for serving at the end of the evening to guests at an Indian party. It acts as a mouth-freshener and coats the mouth with a red coloring.

Poppy seeds
These dried whole seeds are always better when toasted. They are used, often whole, to flavor curries. Although they are from the opium poppy, they do not contain opium.

Raita
A cool dip consisting of yogurt with either onions or cucumber is often served as an accompaniment to hot, spicy dishes.

Rose Water
The essence of roses which is used mainly to flavor Indian sweet dishes. Rose petals are widely used to garnish food as well.

Saffron
This highly valued and expensive spice consists of dried stigma's from a special crocus. Used to flavor rice and sweets, it is only used in very small quantities. Saffron is sold both as strands and in powder form. It has a beautiful flavor and fragrance.

Seasame seeds
Whole, flat, cream-colored seeds, these are used to flavor some curries. When ground they can be made into chutney.

Shallots
The shallot is widely used in Indian cooking along with onions and spring onions. The shallot is suited to the making of flavorings of sauces because of its subtlety of flavor and the way in which its tender flesh cooks to such softness.

Tamarind
This is a pod-like fruit from a tall, shade tree and the dried, or semi-dried pulp is used for cooking. It is usually sold in blocks and to obtain a purée or paste to use in cooking, it has to be soaked in hot water for a couple of hours, then the pulp can be sieved for use. It gives food a sour and slightly sweet flavor. However, commercially produced tamarind paste is widely available now.

Tandoori Masala
A commercially produced Indian spice powder mix which livens up any curry. It can also be used as part of a marinade mixture.

Turmeric
A rhizome, which when dried, results in a bright yellow powder. This musky spice is used in small quantities mainly in vegetable and lentil dishes.

Varq
Edible beaten silver leaf used for decoration purposes. It should be handled gently as it is very light and airy. It can be bought in sheets from Indian or Pakistani grocers.

soups, starters, & snacks

Most of these dishes are usually served as part of a main Indian meal. Here, however, they make easy and elegant starters and snacks. Alternatively, serve with salad and bread for a wonderfully light meal.

Preparation time 10 minutes Cooking time 20 minutes Total time 30 minutes Serves 4

khandvi

4 tbsp. chickpea (gram) flour
1 tbsp. plain yogurt
2 tsp. sea salt
¼ tsp. ground turmeric
¼ tsp. asafetida
1 tsp. chili powder
2 cups water
2 tbsp. sunflower oil
8–10 curry leaves
2 tsp. mustard seeds
1 tbsp. grated fresh coconut
1 tbsp. chopped fresh cilantro

These lightly spiced rolls are the Indian equivalent of pasta, but are made from chickpea flour. Flavored with coconut, cilantro, and mustard seeds, they make a wonderful cold starter.

one In a bowl, whisk together the flour, yogurt, salt, turmeric, asafetida, chili powder, and water.

two Put this mixture in a heavy-based saucepan and bring to a boil, stirring occasionally.

three Lower the heat and cook, stirring frequently, for 10–15 minutes until thick. Remove from the heat.

four Lightly oil a 12 x 12 inch baking sheet and spoon the mixture onto the tray, spreading it thinly over the surface with the back of a wide spoon. Leave for about 5-10 minutes to cool, then cut into 1 inch strips and roll up into mini Swiss rolls. Divide among 4 plates and set aside.

five Heat the oil in a small saucepan and, when hot, add the curry leaves and mustard seeds. As soon as the seeds start to pop, spoon the oil over the rolls. Sprinkle over the coconut and cilantro and serve.

Preparation time 5 minutes Cooking time 15 minutes Total time 20 minutes Serves 4

paneer tikka

1 tbsp. sunflower oil
½ oz. butter
1 tsp. cumin seeds
7 oz. chestnut mushrooms, thinly sliced
8 oz paneer, cut into bite-sized cubes
1 tsp. sea salt
1 tsp. freshly ground black pepper
1 tsp. tandoori masala powder
a handful of chopped cilantro
1 tbsp. lemon juice
shredded iceberg lettuce
mint leaves, to garnish

Ready-prepared paneer is now widely available and can be found in the cheese section of many supermarkets. However, it is simple to make your own (see page 34).

one Heat the oil and butter in a large wok or nonstick frying pan and when hot, add the cumin and mushrooms. Fry, stirring, for 5–7 minutes.

two Add the paneer, salt, pepper, tandoori masala, cilantro, and lemon juice and cook over a low heat, stirring occasionally, for 7–8 minutes.

three To serve, arrange some shredded lettuce on each plate and top with the paneer tikka. Garnish with mint leaves and serve warm.

Preparation time 10 minutes Cooking time 20 minutes Total time 30 minutes Makes 6 pancakes

spiced spinach
and carrot pancakes

3 oz. carrots, grated
3 oz. spinach, coarsely chopped
1 onion, finely chopped
2 fresh green chilies, deseeded and chopped
1 tsp. fennel seeds
1 tbsp. ground coriander
1¾ cups chickpea (gram) flour, sieved
½ cup semolina
1 tsp. baking powder
1 cup water
vegetable oil
sea salt

These pancakes from Gujerat are made from chickpea flour and are known as "pudlas." Serve them as a starter, with Cucumber and Pomegranate Raita (see page 32).

one In a large bowl mix together the carrots, spinach, onion, chilies, fennel seeds, and coriander. Season with salt and set aside.

two Mix together the chickpea flour, semolina, and baking powder and add to the carrot mixture.

three Add the water gradually to the mixture, mixing well with a spoon, until you have a thick batter.

four Lightly grease a nonstick frying pan with oil. When hot, add 2 tbsp. of the mixture and spread with a spatula to make a pancake about 6½–7 inches in diameter. Cover and cook for 1–2 minutes, or until the pancake is lightly browned on the base, then flip over and cook for another 2 minutes. Repeat with the remaining batter to make 6 pancakes. Serve them hot.

Tip: The cooked pancakes can be stored on a lined baking sheet, stacked and interleaved with waxed paper, and kept in a low oven, 225°F, until you are ready to serve them.

Preparation time 10 minutes, plus resting

Cooking time 10 minutes Total time 20 minutes Makes 10-12

onion bhajiyas

1 onion, halved and thinly sliced
5 tbsp. chickpea (gram) flour
1 tbsp. sunflower oil
2 tsp. sea salt
1 tsp. sugar
1 tsp. lemon juice
1 tsp. ground cumin
1 fresh green chili, deseeded and
finely chopped
1 tbsp chopped fresh cilantro
¾ tsp. baking powder
2-3 tbsp. water
vegetable oil, for deep-frying

A popular snack sold on almost every street corner in India, these bhajiyas are delicious served hot with Tamarind and Date Chutney (see page 30) and Coconut Chutney (see page 37).

one Mix all the ingredients together in a bowl (apart from the oil for deep-frying) and let the mixture rest for 10 minutes.

two Using your hands, mix well to combine thoroughly.

three Heat the oil in a wok to 350-375°F, or until a cube of bread browns in 30 seconds, and then drop spoonfuls of the mixture into the oil and deep-fry for 1-2 minutes, until golden. You might have to do this in two or three batches.

four Serve hot with tamarind and date chutney and/or coconut chutney.

Preparation time 10 minutes, plus marinating

Cooking time 4–5 minutes Total time 15 minutes Serves 4

shrimp and mango kebabs

16 large raw tiger shrimp, peeled
and deveined
1 tbsp. sunflower oil
4 tbsp. lemon juice
2 garlic cloves, crushed
1 tsp. grated fresh ginger
1 tsp. chili powder
1 tablespoon honey
1 tsp. sea salt
1 large mango, peeled, pitted and
cut into 8 bite-sized pieces
dressed salad, to serve

These kebabs make a colorful and elegant starter.

one Put the shrimp in a large bowl and add the oil, lemon juice, garlic, ginger, chili powder, honey, and salt. Mix well and marinate for about 10 minutes.

two Remove the shrimp from the marinade and thread 2 shrimp alternately between 2 pieces of mango on each of 8 skewers.

three Place the skewers under a preheated hot grill, brush with the remaining marinade, and grill for 2 minutes on each side, or until the shrimp turn pink and are cooked through.

four Serve 2 skewers on each plate, with some dressed salad.

Preparation time 10 minutes Cooking time 20 minutes Total time 30 minutes Serves 4

coriander chicken kebabs

a handful of coarsely chopped cilantro
2 tbsp. chopped mint leaves
5 garlic cloves, coarsely chopped
2 tsp. grated fresh ginger
1 tsp. ground cumin
1 tsp. ground coriander
1 fresh green chili, coarsely chopped
2 tsp. soft brown sugar
13 oz. minced chicken
1 cup fresh breadcrumbs
sea salt and pepper
lemon wedges, to serve

Serve these delicious kebabs on their own as a starter or with salad for a light lunch.

one Put the chopped cilantro, mint, garlic, ginger, cumin, ground coriander, chili, and sugar in a food processor and process until fairly smooth. Season with salt and pepper.

two Turn the mixture into a large bowl and add the chicken and breadcrumbs. Mix well, using your hands.

three Divide the mixture into 12 and shape around metal or presoaked wooden skewers, using your hands.

four Arrange the kebabs on a wire rack on a baking sheet and bake in a preheated oven, 400°F for 20 minutes.

five Serve hot, with lemon wedges.

Preparation time 15 minutes   Cooking time 15 minutes   Total time 30 minutes   Makes 20

spicy fish cakes

14 oz. cooked cod fillet
2 potatoes, boiled and mashed
4 scallions, thinly sliced
2 fresh green chilies, deseeded and finely chopped
1 tsp. grated fresh ginger
2 garlic cloves, crushed
4 tbsp. chopped fresh cilantro
2 eggs
fresh breadcrumbs, for coating
vegetable oil
sea salt and pepper

Salmon could easily replace the cod in these delicious fish cakes. Serve them with the Kachumber (see page 37) and Mango, Apple, and Mint Chutney (see page 35).

one Flake the fish into a bowl and add the potatoes, scallions, chilies, ginger, garlic, and cilantro. Season with salt and pepper and add 1 egg. Mix well.

two Shape the fish mixture into 20 small cakes and set aside.

three Beat the remaining egg in a shallow bowl, dip the cakes in the egg, and then coat with the breadcrumbs.

four Heat the oil in a large nonstick frying pan and fry the cakes, in batches, for 2 minutes on each side, or until golden brown. Serve hot.

Preparation time 5 minutes Cooking time 6-7 minutes Total time 11-12 minutes Serves 4

akuri

1 tbsp. butter
1 small red onion, finely chopped
1 fresh green chili, finely sliced
8 eggs, lightly beaten
1 tablespoon crème fraîche
1 tomato, finely chopped
1 tablespoon chopped fresh cilantro
sea salt
buttered toast, to serve

These spicy scrambled eggs make a wonderful "pick-me-up" breakfast or an equally good starter, served with hot buttered toast or toasted ciabatta.

one Heat the butter in a large nonstick frying pan and add the onion and chili. Stir-fry for 1–2 minutes.

two Add the eggs, crème fraîche, tomato, and cilantro. Season with salt and cook over a medium-low heat, stirring frequently, for about 3–4 minutes, or until the eggs are lightly scrambled and set. Serve hot with buttered toast.

Preparation time 10 minutes Cooking time 15 minutes Total time 25 minutes Serves 4

tomato and cilantro soup

2 tbsp. sunflower oil
4 scallions
4 curry leaves or 1 bay leaf
13 oz. can chopped tomatoes
1 tsp. sea salt
1 garlic clove, crushed
1 tsp. black peppercorns, coarsely crushed
3 tbsp. chopped fresh cilantro
2 cups. vegetable stock
1 cup light cream
hot crusty bread, to serve

Use homemade or good quality vegetable stock to make this flavorsome soup.

one Heat the oil in a large saucepan and, when hot, add the scallions, curry leaves or bay leaf, and tomatoes and cook over a medium heat for 2–3 minutes.

two Add the salt, garlic, peppercorns, cilantro, and vegetable stock. Stir and bring to a boil. Cover the pan, lower the heat, and simmer gently for 10 minutes.

three Stir in the cream and cook gently for 1–2 minutes.

four Ladle the soup into 4 bowls and serve with hot crusty bread.

Preparation time 10 minutes Cooking time 15-20 minutes Total time 25-30 minutes Makes 12

vegetable samosas

3 large potatoes, boiled and coarsely mashed
3½ oz. cooked peas
1 tsp. cumin seeds
1 tsp. amchoor (dried mango powder)
2 fresh green chilies, deseeded and
finely chopped
1 small red onion, finely chopped
3 tbsp. chopped fresh cilantro
1 tbsp. chopped mint
4 tbsp. lemon juice
12 phyllo pastry sheets, each about
12 x 7 inches
melted butter, for brushing
sea salt and pepper

These crisp savory treats can be made in advance and frozen. They can then be cooked straight from the freezer. Serve with Coconut Chutney (see page 37).

one In a large bowl, mix together the potatoes, peas, cumin, amchoor, chilies, onion, cilantro, mint, and lemon juice. Season with salt and pepper to taste and set aside.

two Fold each sheet of phyllo pastry in half lengthways. Put a large spoonful of the potato mixture at one end and then fold the corner of the pastry over the mixture, covering it in a triangular shape. Continue folding over the triangle of pastry along the length of the pastry strip to make a neat triangular samosa.

three Place the samosas on a baking sheet lined with baking parchment, brush with melted butter, and bake in a preheated oven, 400°F, for 15–20 minutes, or until golden.

salads &
side dishes

These accompaniments of salads, relishes, pickles, and chutneys form an integral part of any Indian meal.

Preparation time 10 minutes Total time 10 minutes Serves 4

chickpea salad

13 oz. can chickpeas, rinsed and drained
½ iceberg lettuce, finely shredded
1 cucumber, finely diced
1 small red onion, halved and thinly sliced
4 plum tomatoes, coarsely chopped
fresh cilantro, to garnish
For the dressing:
1 garlic clove, crushed
1 tbsp. olive oil
2 tbsp. lime juice
1 tsp. sugar
½ tsp. ground cumin
½ tsp. ground coriander

A mildly spiced dressing adds a kick to this nutritious salad.

one Put the chickpeas, lettuce, cucumber, onion, and tomatoes in a wide, shallow serving dish or bowl.

two Mix together the ingredients for the dressing and pour over the salad.

three Toss to mix well and serve garnished with cilantro.

potato and red kidney bean salad

13 oz. potatoes, peeled and cut
into 1 inch cubes
8 oz. Greek yogurt
1 garlic clove, crushed
1 fresh red chili, thinly sliced
1 tsp. honey
2 tbsp. lime juice
4 tbsp. chopped dill
4 scallions, thinly sliced
13 oz. can red kidney beans,
drained and rinsed
sea salt and pepper

This substantial salad is a superb variation on a traditional dish.

one Boil the potatoes in a large pan of water until tender. Drain and set aside.

two In a bowl, mix together the yogurt, garlic, chili, honey, lime juice, and dill. Set aside.

three Transfer the potatoes to a salad bowl and add the scallions and red kidney beans. Pour over the yogurt and dill mixture, season with salt and pepper, and serve at room temperature.

cucumber and pomegranate raita

8 oz. plain yogurt
1 cucumber, peeled, deseeded and
finely chopped
2 tbsp. chopped mint leaves
1 tbsp. chopped fresh cilantro
seeds from ½ pomegranate
sea salt and pepper

This bejeweled raita is the perfect foil to any hot and spicy dish.

one Beat the yogurt in a bowl and add the cucumber, mint, cilantro, and pomegranate seeds. Season with salt and pepper and chill until ready to serve.

Preparation time 10 minutes **Cooking time** 8–10 minutes **Total time** 18–20 minutes **Serves** 4

lobia salad

2 potatoes, cut into small cubes
3½ oz. green beans, cut into
1 inch pieces
13 oz. can black-eyed peas, rinsed and drained
4 scallions, thinly sliced
1 fresh green chili, deseeded and finely chopped
1 tomato, coarsely chopped
a handful of mint leaves
hot, toasted Naan (see page 103), to serve
For the dressing:
2 tbsp. light olive oil
1 tbsp. lemon juice
½ tsp. chili powder
1 tsp. honey
sea salt and pepper

Black-eyed peas feature in this unusual salad.

one Cook the potatoes and green beans in a large pan of boiling water for 8-10 minutes. Drain and place in a large serving bowl.

two Add the black-eyed peas, scallions, chili, tomato, and mint leaves. Toss to mix well.

three Combine all the dressing ingredients in a small bowl and mix well. Pour over the salad, mix well, and serve with hot toasted naan bread.

Preparation time 10 minutes Total time 10 minutes Makes about 7 oz.

tamarind and date chutney

7 oz. pitted dried dates, coarsely chopped
1 tbsp. tamarind paste
1 tsp. ground cumin
1 tsp. chili powder
1 tbsp. tomato ketchup
7 oz. water
sea salt

This sweet-and-sour relish makes a great accompaniment to any Indian meal, but it is wonderful in a cheese sandwich as well.

one Put all the ingredients in a food processor or blender and process until fairly smooth.

two Transfer to a serving bowl, cover, and chill until required. It will keep for up to 3 days in the refrigerator.

Preparation time 5 minutes Total time 5 minutes Makes 8–10

lasan chutney

12 garlic cloves, chopped
1 tsp. chili powder
2 fresh red chilies, chopped
1 tbsp. vegetable oil
1 tsp. sea salt
1 tbsp. lime juice

This spicy accompaniment is not for the fainthearted. It is wonderful with rice dishes and can really spice up a sandwich.

one Put all the ingredients in a food processor or blender and process until smooth. Alternatively, pound to a paste in a mortar with a pestle. This chutney will keep well for up to 2 weeks, stored in an airtight container in the refrigerator.

Preparation time 10 minutes Cooking time 7–8 minutes Total time 17–18 minutes Serves 4

cauliflower relish

2 tbsp. vegetable oil
2 tsp. black mustard seeds
½ tsp. ground turmeric
½ tsp. asafetida
1 small cauliflower, cut into bite-sized pieces
1 red onion, finely chopped
1 fresh green chili, deseeded and
finely chopped
lemon juice
sea salt

This is delicious as an accompaniment to kebabs and samosas.

one Heat the oil in a large nonstick frying pan and, when hot, add the mustard seeds, turmeric, and asafetida. When the seeds start to pop, add the cauliflower, onion, and chili. Stir-fry for 5 minutes and then remove from the heat. The cauliflower should have a bite to it.

two Season with lemon juice and salt to taste. Serve at room temperature.

Preparation time 10 minutes Cooking time 2–3 minutes Total time 12–13 minutes Serves 4

ginger relish

2 tbsp. grated fresh ginger
2 garlic cloves, coarsely chopped
1 tbsp. grated fresh coconut or
2 tbsp. dried coconut
2 fresh green chilies, deseeded
1 tsp. sea salt
1 tsp. sugar
½ cup plain yogurt, beaten
2 tbsp. vegetable oil
1 tsp. black mustard seeds
6-8 curry leaves

This southern Indian relish is a delicious accompaniment to any meal.

one Put the ginger, garlic, coconut, chilies, salt, and sugar in a food processor or blender and process until smooth. Add the yogurt and process for a few seconds.

two Transfer to a bowl and set aside.

three Heat the oil in a small frying pan and add the mustard seeds and curry leaves. When the mustard seeds start to pop, remove the pan from the heat and pour the spiced oil over the yogurt mixture. Mix well and chill until required.

Preparation time 10 minutes Cooking time 2–3 minutes Total time 12–13 minutes Serves 4

gujarati carrot salad

1 lb. carrots, coarsely grated
4 tbsp. lemon juice
1 tbsp. honey
1 tbsp. vegetable oil
½ tsp. dried chili flakes
2 tsp. black mustard seeds
4 curry leaves
sea salt

Hot spicy oil and honey create a delicious sweet-and-sour dressing for this simple salad.

one Place the carrots in a serving bowl.

two Mix together the lemon juice and honey and pour over the carrots. Season with salt.

three Heat the oil in a small saucepan and, when hot, add the chili flakes, mustard seeds, and curry leaves. As soon as the mustard seeds start to pop, remove the pan from the heat and pour the dressing over the carrots. Stir well to mix.

Preparation time 2 minutes **Cooking time** 15–20 minutes, plus setting

Total time 14 minutes **Makes** about 5 oz.

paneer

3 ½ cups whole milk
2 tbsp. lemon juice

This fresh cheese is now widely available from supermarkets, but it is really special and satisfying when made from scratch. Use in the recipe for Paneer Tikka (see page 14) or serve it on hot Naan (see page 103) with a relish or pickle.

one Heat the milk in a large saucepan and bring to the boil.

two Add the lemon juice, stirring continuously, until the milk thickens and then begins to curdle.

three Strain the curdled milk through a fine sieve, discarding the whey.

four Turn the cheese out on to a clean chopping board and sandwich with another clean board. Put a heavy weight on top and let set for 1 hour. Once set, the cheese can be cut or crumbled into other dishes.

lime pickle

10 limes, each cut into 6 sections
3½ oz. sea salt
1 tbsp. fenugreek seeds
1 tbsp. black mustard seeds
1 tbsp. chili powder
1 tbsp. ground turmeric
1 cup vegetable oil
½ tsp. ground asafetida

This pickle is a wonderful accompaniment to rice, yogurt, and a simple dhal.

one Place the limes in a sterilized jar and cover with the salt.

two In a small frying pan, dry-fry the fenugreek and mustard seeds and then grind them to a powder.

three Add the ground seeds, chili powder, and turmeric to the limes and mix well.

four Heat the oil in a small frying pan until smoking, add the asafetida and fry for 30 seconds. Pour the oil over the limes and mix well.

five Cover the jar with a clean cloth and let mature for 10 days in a bright, warm place. Store the pickle in a tightly covered container. This pickle can be kept for a couple of months.

Tip: Grind the spices in a mortar with a pestle, a spice grinder or a coffee grinder kept especially for the purpose.

mango, apple, and mint chutney

1 raw green mango, peeled stoned and coarsely chopped
1 small apple, peeled, cored and coarsely chopped
1 tsp. sea salt
1 tbsp. chopped mint leaves
1 tsp. mild chili powder
1 tsp. soft brown sugar
½ cup water

This relish is a tasty accompaniment to many snacks. Try it with Spicy Fish Cakes (see page 20).

one Put all the ingredients in a food processor or blender and process until smooth.

two Transfer to a small serving dish, cover and store in the refrigerator until required.

cilantro chutney

8 oz. chopped fresh cilantro leaves
and stalks
4 fresh green chilies, deseeded
2 tsp. grated fresh ginger
4 garlic cloves, chopped
2 tsp. sugar
1 tsp. ground cumin
4 tbsp. lemon juice
3 tbsp. chopped mint leaves
7 oz. water
sea salt

This vibrant green chutney is wonderful spread in cucumber sandwiches, adds zing when used as a marinade for grilled fish, and livens up any soup or dhal.

one Put all the ingredients in a food processor or blender and process until smooth.

two Transfer the chutney to a serving bowl and keep covered in the refrigerator until ready to use. It will keep for up to 3–4 days in the refrigerator.

coconut chutney

3½ oz. grated fresh coconut
3 fresh green chilies, deseeded
1 tsp. sugar
2 tsp. grated fresh ginger
½ cup plain yogurt
2 tbsp. vegetable oil
2 tsp. black mustard seeds
6–8 curry leaves
sea salt

This chutney is a terrific accompaniment to Vegetable Samosas (see page 22).

one Put the coconut, chilies, sugar, ginger, and yogurt in a food processor or blender and process until smooth. Transfer to a bowl and set aside.

two Heat the oil in a small frying pan and, when hot, add the mustard seeds and curry leaves. As soon as the seeds start to pop, remove the pan from the heat and pour the spicy oil over the yogurt mixture. Season with salt to taste. Chill until ready to serve.

kachumber

1 red onion, halved and thinly sliced
2 ripe plum tomatoes, finely chopped
1 small cucumber, peeled and finely chopped
1 fresh green chili, deseeded and thinly sliced
a handful of chopped fresh cilantro
4 tbsp. lemon juice
½ tsp. sugar
sea salt and pepper

Tomatoes, onion, and cucumber feature in this traditional and refreshing salad.

one Mix all the ingredients in a bowl, season with salt and pepper, and allow to rest for at least 15 minutes before serving.

meat & poultry

Yogurt is used widely in India for marinating meat and poultry. The yogurt tenderizes the meat and gives a silken texture and wonderful flavor when coupled with other spices and herbs.

Preparation time 10 minutes, plus marinating (optional)

Cooking time 20 minutes Total time 30 minutes Serves 4

tandoori chicken

4 large chicken quarters, skinned
7 oz. plain yogurt
1 tsp. grated fresh ginger
2 garlic cloves, crushed
1 tsp. garam masala
2 tsp. ground coriander
¼ tsp. ground turmeric
1 tbsp. tandoori masala
4 tbsp. lemon juice
1 tbsp. vegetable oil
sea salt
lime or lemon wedges, to garnish

The flavor of this chicken dish when cooked in a tandoor (clay oven) is sublime. However, this recipe comes very close to capturing the real thing.

one Place the chicken in a nonmetallic, shallow, ovenproof dish and make 3 deep slashes in each piece, to allow the flavors to penetrate. Set aside.

two Mix together the yogurt, ginger, garlic, garam masala, ground coriander, turmeric, tandoori masala, lemon juice, and oil. Season with salt and spread over the chicken pieces to cover. Cover and marinate overnight in the refrigerator, if time allows.

three Bake the chicken in a preheated oven 475°F for 20 minutes, or until cooked through. Remove from the oven and serve hot, garnished with lime or lemon wedges.

Preparation time 10 minutes Cooking time 15 minutes Total time 25 minutes Serves 4

ginger chicken

8 oz. plain yogurt
1 tbsp. grated fresh ginger
2 garlic cloves, crushed
1 tbsp. chili powder
1 tbsp. ground coriander
2 tsp. ground cumin
2 tbsp. vegetable oil
8 oz. chicken thighs, skinned, boned, and cut into bite-sized pieces
½ cup chicken stock
sea salt and pepper
chopped fresh cilantro, to garnish

one In a bowl, mix together the yogurt, ginger, garlic, chili powder, ground coriander, and cumin. Season with salt and pepper.

two Heat the oil in a large nonstick frying pan and, when hot, add the chicken. Stir-fry for 4–5 minutes, or until sealed.

three Add the yogurt mixture and the stock. Bring to the boil, cover, and cook gently for 8–10 minutes, stirring frequently, until the chicken is tender and cooked through. Serve hot, garnished with chopped cilantro

chettinad chicken

2 tbsp. sunflower oil
1 onion, halved and thinly sliced
10 curry leaves
1 fresh green chili, chopped
2 garlic cloves, crushed
2 tsp. grated fresh ginger
1 tsp. ground coriander
14½ oz. chicken thighs, skinned, boned, and
cut into bite-sized pieces
8 oz. chicken stock
1 tsp. garam masala
sea salt and pepper

This dish comes from southern India and should be eaten with rice and yogurt.

one Heat the oil in a large nonstick frying pan and, when hot, add the onion, curry leaves, and chili. Fry, stirring constantly, until the onions are soft. Add the garlic and ginger and stir-fry for 1–2 minutes.

two Add the ground coriander and chicken and fry, stirring constantly, for 2–3 minutes. Pour in the stock and add the garam masala. Cover and cook gently for 10–12 minutes, or until the chicken is cooked through. Season with salt and pepper and serve hot.

cashew nut chicken

1 onion, coarsely chopped
4 tbsp. tomato purée
½ cup cashew nuts
2 tsp. garam masala
2 garlic cloves, crushed
1 tbsp. lemon juice
¼ tsp. ground turmeric
2 tsp. sea salt
1 tbsp. plain yogurt
2 tbsp. vegetable oil
3 tbsp. chopped fresh cilantro
½ cup dried apricots, chopped
1 lb. chicken thighs, skinned, boned, and cut into bite-sized pieces
1 cup chicken stock
toasted cashew nuts and chopped fresh cilantro, to garnish

Cashew nuts form the basis of this lovely thick and nutty curry.

one Put the onion, tomato purée, cashews, garam masala, garlic, lemon juice, turmeric, salt, and yogurt into a food processor or blender and process until fairly smooth. Set aside.

two Heat the oil in a large nonstick frying pan and, when hot, pour in the spice mixture. Fry, stirring, for 2 minutes over a medium heat. Add half the cilantro leaves, the apricots, and chicken to the pan and stir-fry for 1 minute.

three Pour in the stock, cover and simmer for 10–12 minutes, or until the chicken is cooked through and tender. Stir in the remaining cilantro leaves and serve garnished with toasted cashew nuts and chopped cilantro.

Preparation time 10 minutes Cooking time 15 minutes Total time 25 minutes Serves 4

bombay chicken masala

1 onion, coarsely chopped
6 fresh green chilies, deseeded and chopped
6 garlic cloves, chopped
2 tsp. grated fresh ginger
1 tbsp. ground coriander
2 tsp. ground cumin
a large bunch of fresh cilantro,
coarsely chopped
½ cup water
2 tbsp. vegetable oil
13 oz. boneless chicken breast, cut into strips
8 oz. chicken stock
sea salt and pepper

This is an excellent dish for a family supper or a midweek meal with friends.

one Put the onion, chilies, garlic, ginger, ground coriander, cumin, cilantro, and water in a food processor or blender; process to a fairly smooth green paste. Set aside.

two Heat the oil in a large nonstick frying pan and add the green paste. Fry, stirring constantly, for 1 minute and then add the chicken. Fry, stirring, for 2–3 minutes, then add the stock. Mix well, cover, and cook gently for 10–12 minutes, or until the chicken is tender. Season with salt and pepper and serve hot.

chicken achaari

2 tbsp. vegetable oil
½ tsp. cumin seeds
½ tsp. black mustard seeds
½ tsp. onion seeds
½ tsp. fennel seeds
½ tsp. coriander seeds
1 tsp. grated fresh ginger
2 garlic cloves, finely chopped
1 onion, finely chopped
1 tsp. chili powder
7 oz. chicken stock
2 tbsp. tomato purée
8 oz. chicken thighs, skinned, boned, and
cut into bite-sized pieces
sea salt and pepper
chopped fresh red chilies, to garnish

The spices used in this dish are usually associated with making pickles "achaar," hence the name.

one Heat the oil in a wok or large frying pan. When hot, add the cumin, mustard seeds, onion seeds, fennel, and coriander seeds and stir-fry for 1 minute.

two Add the ginger, garlic, onion, chili powder, stock, and tomato purée and stir for 1 minute.

three Add the chicken and bring to the boil. Lower the heat, cover the pan and simmer for 5–7 minutes, or until the chicken is tender and cooked through. Season with salt and pepper and garnish with the chopped chilies.

coconut chicken

1 tbsp. ground almonds
1 tbsp. dried coconut
½ cup coconut milk
½ cup fromage frais
2 tsp. ground coriander
1 tsp. chili powder
2 garlic cloves, crushed
2 tsp. grated fresh ginger
2 tsp. sea salt
1 tbsp. vegetable oil
13 oz. chicken thighs, skinned, boned, and cut
into bite-sized pieces
4 cardamom pods
1 tsp. crushed red chili flakes
3 tbsp. chopped fresh cilantro
plain boiled rice, to serve

Both coconut milk and flesh enrich the flavor of this delicately spiced dish.

one In a small frying pan, dry-fry the almonds and coconut, stirring constantly, until light brown. Transfer to a mixing bowl and add the coconut milk, fromage frais, ground coriander, chili powder, garlic, ginger, and salt. Stir to mix well.

two Heat the oil in a large nonstick frying pan and sauté the chicken and cardamom for 2–3 minutes.

three Stir in the coconut mixture and chili flakes, cover and cook gently for 10–12 minutes, stirring occasionally. Add the chopped cilantro, stir and serve hot, with plain boiled rice.

Preparation time 10 minutes Cooking time 15–20 minutes Total time 25–30 minutes Serves 4

kheema aloo

1 tbsp. vegetable oil
4 cardamom pods
1 cinnamon stick
3 cloves
2 onions, finely chopped
12 oz. ground lamb
2 tsp. garam masala
2 tsp. chili powder
2 garlic cloves, crushed
2 tsp. grated fresh ginger
2 tsp. sea salt
7 oz. potatoes, cut into
½ inch cubes
7 oz. can chopped tomatoes
½ cup hot water
4 tbsp. chopped fresh cilantro
boiled rice or bread, to serve

This spicy, ground lamb dish with potatoes is gently flavored with cardamom, cinnamon, and cloves. Ground lamb may be replaced with ground chicken or pork.

one Heat the oil in a nonstick frying pan and, when hot, add the cardamom pods, cinnamon, and cloves. Fry for 1 minute and then add the onion and fry, stirring, for 3–4 minutes.

two Add the lamb to the pan with the garam masala, chili powder, garlic, ginger, and salt. Stir well to break up the pieces and fry for 5–7 minutes.

three Add the potatoes, tomatoes, and the measured hot water, cover and simmer gently for 5 minutes, or until the potatoes are tender. Stir in the cilantro and serve hot with rice.

Preparation time 10 minutes, plus chilling (optional)

Cooking time 10 minutes Total time 20 minutes Makes 12

seekh kebabs

2 fresh green chilies, deseeded and
finely chopped
1 tsp. grated fresh ginger
2 garlic cloves, crushed
3 tbsp. chopped fresh cilantro
2 tbsp. chopped mint leaves
1 tsp. cumin seeds
1 tbsp. vegetable oil
½ tsp. ground cloves
½ tsp. ground cardamom seeds
14½ oz. ground beef
sea salt

These kebabs are a popular street food in India. Barbecued over charcoal braziers, they are eaten with red onions, mint, and hot bread.

one Put the chilies, ginger, garlic, cilantro, mint, cumin, oil, ground cloves, and cardamom into a food processor or blender and process until fairly smooth. Transfer to a mixing bowl, add the beef and salt and mix well, using your hands. Divide the mixture into 12 portions, cover, and chill for 30 minutes, if time allows.

two Lightly oil 12 flat metal skewers and shape the kebab mixture around each skewer, forming a sausage shape.

three Place the kebabs under a preheated hot broiler and cook for 3–4 minutes on each side, or until cooked through and browned.

Preparation time 10 minutes, plus marinating (optional)

Cooking time 8–12 minutes **Total time** 18–22 minutes **Serves** 4

kashmiri lamb chops

½ cup plain yogurt
1 tsp. chili powder
2 tsp. grated fresh ginger
2 garlic cloves, crushed
1 tbsp. sunflower oil, plus extra for oiling
8 lamb loin chops
sea salt and pepper

one Mix together the yogurt, chili powder, ginger, garlic, and oil in a large bowl and season with salt and pepper.

two Add the chops to this mixture and coat them thoroughly. Cover and marinate for 3–10 hours in the refrigerator, if time allows.

three Place the chops on a lightly oiled broiler pan. Cook under a preheated hot broiler for 4–6 minutes on each side, or until tender.

Preparation time 10 minutes **Cooking time** 20 minutes **Total time** 30 minutes **Makes** 12

lamb kebabs

14½ oz. ground lamb
1 small red onion, finely chopped
3 tbsp. chopped fresh cilantro
2 tbsp. chopped mint leaves
2 fresh green chilies, chopped
2 garlic cloves, crushed
2 tsp. grated fresh ginger
1 egg, lightly beaten
sea salt and pepper

These kebabs are a spicy alternative to the hamburger. They work wonderfully stuffed in pita bread with salad and could be cooked on a barbecue.

one Line a baking sheet with baking parchment and set aside.

two Place the lamb, onion, cilantro, mint, chilies, garlic, ginger, and egg in a large bowl, season with salt and pepper and, using your hands, mix until thoroughly blended. Divide the mixture into 12 portions and form each one into a round shape.

three Place the kebabs on the baking sheet and bake in a preheated oven, 400°F, for 20 minutes, or until golden brown. Serve hot.

beef chili fry

3 tbsp. vegetable oil
6 large fresh green chilies, slit in half
1 tsp. cumin seeds
4 curry leaves
2 tsp. grated fresh ginger
1 tsp. chili powder
1 tsp. ground coriander
2 garlic cloves, crushed
2 tsp. sea salt
2 onions, finely chopped
14½ oz. beef sirloin steak, cut into thin strips
4 tbsp. lemon juice
2 tbsp. chopped mint
1 tbsp. chopped fresh cilantro

one Heat the oil in a large nonstick frying pan and, when hot, add the chilies. Fry for 1 minute and then remove with a slotted spoon and set aside.

two Add the cumin, curry leaves, ginger, chili powder, ground coriander, garlic, salt, and onions to the pan and stir-fry for 1-2 minutes, stirring continuously.

three Add the beef strips and stir-fry for 8-10 minutes, until cooked through.

four Add the lemon juice, mint, and chopped cilantro, return the green chilies to the pan and fry, stirring, for 1-2 minutes. Serve immediately.

Preparation time 10 minutes, plus chilling Cooking time 6–8 minutes

Total time 16–18 minutes Makes 12

spicy pork patties

14½ oz. ground pork
3 tsp. hot curry paste
3 tbsp. fresh breadcrumbs
1 small onion, finely chopped
2 tbsp. lime juice
2 tbsp. chopped fresh cilantro
1 fresh red chili, finely chopped
2 tsp. soft brown sugar
sunflower oil
sea salt and pepper
To serve:
plain yogurt
kachumber (see page 37)

one Put the pork, curry paste, breadcrumbs, onion, lime juice, cilantro, chili, and sugar into a large bowl and, using your hands, mix until thoroughly blended. Season with salt and pepper, cover and chill for 30 minutes, or until ready to cook.

two Divide the mixture into 12 portions and shape each one into a flat round patty.

three Heat the oil in a large nonstick frying pan and cook the patties over a moderate heat for 3–4 minutes on each side, or until cooked through. Remove with a slotted spoon and drain on paper.towels Serve hot, with yogurt and kachumber.

fish &
shellfish

Healthy, delicious, and
really quick to cook,
these seafood recipes
are influenced by the
various different coastal
regions of India.

Preparation time 10 minutes Cooking time 15 minutes Total time 25 minutes Serves 4

salmon in banana leaves

a large bunch of fresh cilantro,
coarsely chopped
3 tbsp. chopped mint leaves
2 garlic cloves, crushed
1 tsp. grated fresh ginger
4 fresh red chilies, chopped
2 tsp. ground cumin
1 tsp. ground coriander
2 tsp. soft brown sugar
2 tbsp. lime juice
½ cup coconut milk
4 thick salmon fillets, skinned
4 squares of banana leaf (each
approximately 12 x 12 inches)
sea salt and pepper

All the aromas of the herbs and spices are unleashed when you open up the banana leaf packages.

one Place the chopped coriander, mint, garlic, ginger, chilies, cumin, ground coriander, sugar, lime juice, and coconut milk in a food processor and blend until fairly smooth. Season with salt and pepper and set aside.

two Place each salmon fillet on a square of banana leaf and spoon some of the herb and spice mixture over it. Carefully cover the fish with the leaf to make a neat parcel and secure with wooden skewers.

three Place the parcels on a large baking sheet and bake in a preheated oven, 400°F, for 15 minutes.

four Remove the parcels from the oven, place on a serving plate, and open the packages at the table.

Tip: To make the banana leaves supple, hold them over an open flame until they turn a bright green. They will be supple and easier to handle. If you cannot get banana leaves, use baking parchment instead.

Preparation time 10 minutes Cooking time 15–20 minutes Total time 25–30 minutes Serves 4

spicy pan-fried cod

2 tbsp. chickpea (gram) flour
1 tbsp. all-purpose flour
1 tbsp. amchoor (dried mango powder)
2 tsp. chili powder
1 tbsp. cumin seeds
1 tsp. grated fresh ginger
1 garlic clove, crushed
2 tsp. sea salt
4 thick cod fillets, skinned
sunflower oil

In India, this dish would be prepared with a tropical fish, such as pomfret, but it is also a tasty way to cook cod.

one In a bowl, mix together the flours, amchoor, chili powder, cumin seeds, ginger, garlic, and salt.

two Place the fish on a chopping board and dust with the spiced flour on both sides, to coat evenly.

three Heat the oil in a large nonstick frying pan and, when hot, fry the fish in 2 batches, for 3–4 minutes on each side, or until cooked through. Drain on kitchen paper and serve hot.

Preparation time 10 minutes Cooking time 15 minutes Total time 25 minutes Serves 4

fish mollee

1¾ lb. thick, skinless cod or halibut fillets, cut into 1½ inch pieces
4 tbsp. lemon juice
1 tbsp. vegetable oil
1 onion, finely chopped
3 garlic cloves, crushed
1 tsp. ground turmeric
4 fresh green chilies, deseeded and
1 cup coconut milk
1 tbsp. white wine vinegar
sea salt and pepper

This mild Anglo-Indian curry is wonderful served with boiled rice, Lime Pickle (see page 35), and poppadoms.

one Place the fish in a large, shallow non-metallic dish and sprinkle with salt and the lemon juice. Cover and set aside.

two Heat the oil in a large nonstick frying pan and add the onion and garlic. Fry, stirring constantly, for 2–3 minutes and then add the turmeric, chilies and coconut milk. Cook briskly for 2–3 minutes.

three Add the fish. Stir carefully and add the vinegar. Cover the pan and cook for 7–10 minutes, or until the fish is cooked through. Season with salt and pepper and serve hot.

Variation: Substitute raw tiger shrimp for the fish. Cook until the shrimp have just turned pink.

crab malabar-hill

2 tbsp. vegetable oil
3 garlic cloves, finely chopped
2 tsp. finely chopped fresh ginger
6 scallions, very thinly sliced
3 fresh red chilies, deseeded and finely sliced
1¼ lb. fresh white crabmeat
grated rind and juice of 1 lime
4 tbsp. chopped fresh cilantro
2 tbsp. chopped mint leaves
sea salt and pepper
lettuce leaves, to serve

This dish featured regularly on the menu at my home in Malabar-hill, Bombay.

one Heat the oil in a large wok or nonstick frying pan and, when hot, add the garlic, ginger, scallions, and chilies. Fry, stirring constantly, for 2–3 minutes.

two Add the crabmeat, lime rind and juice, cilantro, and mint. Stir-fry for 2–3 minutes, season with salt and pepper and serve hot on crisp lettuce leaves.

Preparation time 10 minutes Cooking time 15 minutes Total time 25 minutes Serves 4

baked coconut trout

4 small trout, gutted and cleaned
4 tbsp. lemon juice
2 garlic cloves, crushed
1 tsp. grated fresh ginger
1 tbsp. ground almonds
3 tbsp. tomato purée
2 fresh green chilies, finely chopped
1 tsp. garam masala
1 cup coconut milk
1 tbsp. chopped fresh cilantro
1 tbsp. vegetable oil
sea salt and pepper
boiled rice and salad, to serve

one Place the fish in a large, nonmetallic ovenproof dish, season with salt and squeeze over the lemon juice.

two Mix together the garlic, ginger, almonds, tomato purée, chilies, garam masala, coconut milk, cilantro, and oil. Season with salt and pepper and pour over the fish to coat well.

three Bake the fish in a preheated oven, 400°F, for 15 minutes, until it is cooked through. Serve hot with rice and a salad.

Preparation time 10 minutes, plus marinating (optional)

Cooking time 12 minutes **Total time** 22 minutes **Serves** 4

kerala-style fried fish

1 small onion, finely grated to a paste
2 garlic cloves, finely grated
2 tsp. ground coriander
1 tsp. hot chili powder
1 tsp. pepper
1 tbsp. lemon juice
2 tsp. sea salt
1 tbsp. sunflower oil, plus extra for frying
4 skinless flounder fillets
1 cup all-purpose flour
sunflower oil, for frying

My idea of heaven would be sitting under the palms, by the sea, and making a meal of this fried fish, with dhal, rice, and a salad.

one Place the onion, garlic, coriander, chili powder, pepper, lemon juice, salt, and the 1 tbsp. of oil in a bowl and mix thoroughly to form a paste. Place the fish in a large, nonmetallic shallow dish and smear with the paste to coat evenly. Cover and marinate for 1 hour in the refrigerator, if time allows.

two Place the flour on a large plate and, when ready to cook, dredge the fish fillets in it. Shake off any excess flour.

three Heat the oil in a large nonstick frying pan and pan-fry the fish, in batches, for about 2–3 minutes on each side. Drain on paper towels and serve hot.

Preparation time 10 minutes Cooking time 10–12 minutes Total time 20–22 minutes Serves 4

spiced mussel curry

2 lbs. live mussels
1 tbsp. vegetable oil
1 onion, finely chopped
4 garlic cloves, crushed
3 fresh green chilies, finely chopped
1 tsp. ground turmeric
½ cup white wine vinegar
2 cups coconut milk
2 tsp. sugar
4 tbsp. chopped fresh cilantro
sea salt
freshly grated coconut, to garnish
crusty white bread, to serve

This is best made with live mussels, available from supermarkets and fish markets.

one Rinse the mussels under cold, running water and scrape off any beards. Discard any that are open or that do not close when sharply tapped. Drain and set aside.

two Heat the oil in a large saucepan and add the onion, garlic, chilies, and turmeric and fry for 2–3 minutes. Add the mussels, vinegar, coconut milk, sugar, and chopped cilantro. Stir well, bring to the boil, cover, and cook gently for 5–6 minutes, or until all the mussels have opened. Discard any that remain closed.

three With a slotted spoon transfer the mussels into a serving bowl, season sauce to taste, and pour over the mussels. Garnish with grated coconut and eat with crusty white bread to mop up the juices.

shrimp with curry leaves and fenugreek

1 tbsp. sunflower oil
2 onions, halved and thinly sliced
8–10 curry leaves
1 tsp. nigella
1 fresh red chili, finely sliced
1¼ lbs. raw tiger shrimp, peeled and deveined
2 tsp. grated fresh ginger
2 tsp. sea salt
1 tbsp. fenugreek leaves
1 tbsp. lemon juice
hot white bread, to serve

The marriage of the aromatic curry leaves and pungent fresh fenugreek leaves gives this shrimp curry a distinctive flavor.

one Heat the oil in a large nonstick frying pan and add the onions, curry leaves, and nigella and stir-fry for 3 minutes.

two Add the chili and shrimp and fry, stirring constantly, for 5–7 minutes. Add the ginger and salt and fry, stirring, for another minute, or until the shrimp turn pink and are just cooked through.

three Finally, add the fenugreek leaves and lemon juice and cook for 1–2 minutes. Remove from the heat and serve hot with hot white bread.

Preparation time 10 minutes, plus marinating

Cooking time 8–10 minutes Total time 18–20 minutes Serves 4

monkfish kebabs

2 lb. monkfish fillet, cut into
1½ inch cubes
7 oz. plain yogurt
4 tbsp. lemon juice
3 garlic cloves, crushed
2 tsp. grated fresh ginger
1 tsp. hot chili powder
1 tsp. ground cumin
1 tsp. ground coriander
2 fresh red chilies, finely sliced
sea salt and pepper
To garnish:
chopped fresh cilantro
sliced red chilies
lime slices

Monkfish is quite meaty and holds its shape well when cooked, so it is perfect for kebabs.

one Place the monkfish cubes in a bowl and set aside.

two In a small bowl, mix together the yogurt, lemon juice, garlic, ginger, chili powder, cumin, coriander, and chilies and season with salt and pepper. Pour this over the fish, cover, and marinate overnight.

three Lift the fish out of the marinade and thread on to 8 flat metal skewers. Place on a broiler rack and cook under a preheated broiler for 8–10 minutes, turning once, until the fish is cooked through. Serve hot and garnish with chopped cilantro, lime slices, and chili slices.

Preparation time 10 minutes, plus marinating (optional)

Cooking time 20 minutes Total time 30 minutes Serves 4

baked spiced halibut

4 thick halibut steaks (about 7 oz. each)
1 small onion, finely chopped
2 garlic cloves, crushed
1 tsp. grated fresh ginger
2 tsp. ground cumin
1 tsp. ground coriander
4 tbsp. lemon juice
1 tsp. dried red chili flakes
8 oz. plain yogurt
sea salt and pepper
To garnish
lemon wedges and cilantro leaves

one Place the halibut steaks in a large, shallow ovenproof dish and set aside.

two Put the onion, garlic, ginger, cumin, coriander, lemon juice, and chili flakes in a food processor or blender with half the yogurt, and process until smooth. Add the remaining yogurt and blend again. Season with salt and pepper.

three Pour the yogurt marinade over the fish, using your hands to coat the fish thoroughly on both sides. Cover and marinate in the refrigerator overnight, if time allows.

four Cover the dish with foil and bake in a preheated oven, 375°F, for 10 minutes, then remove the foil and bake for another 7–10 minutes, or until the fish is cooked through. Serve hot, garnished with lemon wedges and cilantro leaves.

Preparation time 10 minutes Cooking time 15 minutes Total time 25 minutes Serves 4

tomato fish curry

2 tbsp. vegetable oil
1 onion, finely chopped
4 garlic cloves, sliced
1 tsp. grated fresh ginger
½ tsp. ground turmeric
1 tsp. chili powder
1 tsp. ground cumin
2 tsp. ground coriander
1 tsp. garam masala
1 lb. thick white fish fillets, cut into
1 inch pieces
13 oz. can chopped tomatoes
2 tsp. sea salt
2 tsp. sugar
boiled rice, to serve

Any firm white fish, such as cod or haddock, is suitable for this aromatic curry.

one Heat the oil in a large nonstick frying pan and fry the onion until soft and lightly browned. Add the garlic, ginger, turmeric, chili powder, cumin, coriander, and garam masala and fry for 30 seconds.

two Add the fish and stir gently for 1 minute.

three Add the tomatoes, salt, and sugar. Stir carefully, cover, and simmer gently for 7–10 minutes, or until the fish is cooked through. Serve hot with rice.

Preparation time 10 minutes Cooking time 20 minutes Total time 30 minutes Serves 4

shrimp dopiaza

2 tbsp. vegetable oil
3 onions, thinly sliced
1 tsp. onion seeds
1 tsp. grated garlic
1 tsp. grated fresh ginger
1 tsp. chili powder
½ tsp. ground turmeric
1¼ lb. raw tiger shrimp, peeled and deveined
2 tbsp. fresh cilantro leaves
1 tbsp. lemon juice
sea salt and pepper

Cooked with lots of onions, dopiaza has a rich and spicy flavor.

one Heat the oil in a large nonstick frying pan and add the onions. Cook over a medium heat, stirring occasionally, for about 7–10 minutes, until golden brown.

two Add the onion seeds, garlic, ginger, chili powder, and turmeric, and stir-fry for 1–2 minutes.

three Add the shrimp, cilantro, and lemon juice, and season with salt and pepper. Cover the pan and cook gently for 5–7 minutes, or until the shrimp are cooked through. Serve hot.

Preparation time 10 minutes   Cooking time 15 minutes   Total time 25 minutes   Serves 4

goan shrimp curry

1 tsp. chili powder
1 tbsp. paprika
½ tsp. ground turmeric
4 garlic cloves, crushed
2 tsp. grated fresh ginger
2 tbsp. ground coriander
1 tsp. ground cumin
2 tsp. palm sugar (jaggery) or
soft brown sugar
1 cup water
2 cups coconut milk
2 tsp. sea salt
1 tbsp. tamarind paste
1¼ lb. raw tiger shrimp
boiled white rice, to serve

I prepared a version of this extremely simple and wonderful recipe on a boat off the Goan coast for one of Madhur Jaffrey's television series. I have cooked it regularly since then.

one Put the chili powder, paprika, turmeric, garlic, ginger, ground coriander, cumin, the palm or brown sugar, and the water in a bowl. Mix well and transfer to a large saucepan. Bring this mixture to a boil, cover, and simmer gently for 7–8 minutes.

two Add the coconut milk, salt, and tamarind paste and bring to a simmer.

three Stir in the shrimp and cook briskly until they turn pink and are just cooked through. Serve hot, garnished with chopped cilantro and accompanied by boiled white rice.

Tip: Peel and devein most of the shrimp, leaving just the tail shell in place, but leave a few in their shells to improve the presentation of the dish.

vegetables & legumes

Fresh vegetables and legumes form the
basis of day-to-day Indian cooking.
A wide variety of common and
slightly unusual vegetables are
used in these recipes.

Preparation time 5 minutes, plus soaking

Cooking time 25 minutes Total time 30 minutes Serves 4

tarka dhal

2 cups red split lentils
3½ cups hot water
7 oz. canned chopped tomatoes
2 fresh green chilies, deseeded and
finely chopped (optional)
¼ tsp. ground turmeric
2 tsp. grated fresh ginger
4 tbsp. chopped fresh cilantro
sea salt and pepper
For the tarka:
1 tbsp. sunflower oil
2 tsp. black mustard seeds
1 tsp. cumin seeds
2 garlic cloves, thinly sliced
1 dried red chili

This is the ultimate basic Indian comfort food. Tarka is the process by which food is given the final seasoning, in this case with spiced oil, to flavor the dish. I love to eat this dhal with basmati rice, plain yogurt, and hot green mango pickle or Lime Pickle (see page 35).

one Soak the lentils in boiling water to cover for 10 minutes. Drain and put in a large saucepan with the hot water. Bring to the boil over a high heat, spooning off any scum that comes to the surface. Reduce the heat and cook for 20 minutes, or until soft and tender.

two Drain the lentils and process to a purée in a food processor or using a hand-held electric beater. Return the purée to the rinsed pan with the tomatoes, chilies, turmeric, ginger, and cilantro. Season with salt and pepper, return to the heat and simmer gently.

three Meanwhile, make the tarka. Heat the oil in a small nonstick frying pan and, when hot, add all the ingredients and fry, stirring constantly, for 1–2 minutes.

four Remove the tarka from the heat and pour on to the cooked dhal. Stir and serve hot.

Preparation time 5 minutes Cooking time 20 minutes Total time 25 minutes Serves 4

spinach with besan

1 tbsp. vegetable oil
1 tsp. mustard seeds
2 garlic cloves, finely chopped
8 oz. baby spinach
1 tsp. chili powder
1 tsp. ground cumin
2 tsp. ground coriander
1 fresh green chili, chopped
2 tbsp. besan
4 tbsp. water
dash of lemon juice
sea salt

one Heat the oil in a large frying pan and, when hot, add the mustard seeds, garlic, and spinach. Sauté for 5 minutes and then add the chili powder, cumin, cilantro, and chili.

two Mix together the chickpea flour and water and pour into the spinach mixture. Stir and cook for 5 minutes, until the spinach and chickpea flour are well blended. Cover and cook gently for another 8–10 minutes.

three Season with salt and squeeze over some lemon juice. Serve hot.

Besan is another name for gram or chickpea flour.

Preparation time 10 minutes, plus resting

Cooking time 15–18 minutes **Total time** 25–28 minutes **Serves** 4

stuffed spiced okra

8 oz. large fresh okra, trimmed
1 tsp. grated fresh ginger
1 tsp. ground cumin
1 tbsp. amchoor (dried mango powder)
½ tsp. chili powder
¼ tsp. ground turmeric
2 tsp. vegetable oil
3 tbsp. cornstarch
sea salt and pepper
vegetable oil, for deep-frying

This unusual accompaniment would go as well with Western barbecues as it does with other Indian dishes.

one With a sharp knife, make a lengthways slit in each okra, being careful not to cut right through.

two In a small bowl, mix together the ginger, cumin, amchoor, chili powder, and turmeric. Add the oil, season with salt and pepper, and stir to mix well. Set aside for 10–15 minutes to rest.

three Using your finger and a small teaspoon, carefully part the slits in the okra and fill each one with some of the spiced filling.

four Put the okra into a plastic bag with the cornstarch and shake gently to coat them evenly.

five Pour at least 1½ inches of oil into a wok or deep frying pan and heat. When hot, deep-fry the okra in 3 batches, for about 5–6 minutes, or until they are lightly browned and crisp. Drain on paper towels and serve hot.

Tip: Known as bhindi in India, okra are the seedpods of a member of the hibiscus family. Choose bright green, firm specimens with no signs of browning.

mutter paneer

2 tbsp. vegetable oil
1 tsp. mustard seeds
1 tsp. cumin seeds
1 cinnamon stick or piece of cassia bark
1 dried red Kashmiri chili
4 cloves
4 cardamom pods
1 onion, finely chopped
2 tsp. freshly grated ginger
1 fresh green chili, chopped
4 garlic cloves, crushed
1 tsp. hot chili powder
1 tsp. garam masala
1 tsp. ground turmeric
2 tbsp. dhanajeera (coriander and cumin powder)
2 tsp. brown sugar or palm sugar (jaggery)
7 oz. can chopped tomatoes
2 cups paneer, cubed or crumbled
14½ oz. frozen peas
¾ cup water
4 tbsp. crème fraîche
sea salt
fresh cilantro to garnish

This famous, rich Mogul dish is wonderful when made with freshly made Paneer (see page 34). If pressed for time, you can use the store-bought variety. Do not be intimidated by the long list of spices; if you have everything measured and laid out, it's simple.

one Heat the oil in a large saucepan and when hot, add the mustard and cumin seeds, cinnamon or cassia bark, dried red chili, cloves, and cardamom. Stir-fry until the seeds start to pop and then add the onion and stir-fry for 4–5 minutes. Add the ginger, chili, garlic, chili powder, garam masala, turmeric, dhanajeera, and brown sugar and stir well.

two Add the tomatoes, paneer, peas, and water. Simmer gently for 10 minutes, stirring occasionally.

three Stir in the crème fraîche and season with salt and pepper. Serve hot, garnished with cilantro leaves.

coconut and potato curry

2 tbsp. vegetable oil
2 tsp. black mustard seeds
¼ tsp. asafetida
8–10 curry leaves
1 tsp. grated fresh ginger
1 fresh green chili, chopped
1 lb. potatoes, cut into 1 inch cubes and boiled
1 tsp. hot chili powder
1 tbsp. palm sugar (jaggery)
1 cup coconut milk
1 cup water
1 tbsp. tamarind paste
2 tbsp. roasted cashew nuts, coarsely chopped
3 tbsp. chopped fresh cilantro
sea salt and pepper

This fragrant, sweet, sour, and spicy curry is flavored with tamarind paste, palm sugar, asafetida, and curry leaves. If thinned down with some water, it also makes a great soup.

one Heat the oil in a large frying pan and, when hot, add the mustard seeds, asafetida, curry leaves, ginger, and chili. Stir-fry for 1 minute and add the potatoes. Sauté for 1 minute.

two Sprinkle in the chili powder and add the palm sugar, coconut milk, and water. Bring to the boil and add the tamarind paste and cashews. Lower the heat and simmer for 10–12 minutes. Stir in the cilantro leaves, season with salt and pepper, and serve hot.

Tip: If you cannot find jaggery, use brown sugar.

Preparation time 10 minutes Cooking time 20 minutes Total time 30 minutes Serves 4

oopma

1½ cups coarse semolina
3 tbsp. vegetable oil
1 tsp. black mustard seeds
1 tsp. cumin seeds
1 dried red chili, chopped
10-12 curry leaves
1 red onion, finely chopped
1 fresh green chili, deseeded and chopped
½ cup raisins
2 tbsp. roasted cashew nuts
2 oz. frozen peas
2 cups hot water
1 tbsp. lemon juice
2 tbsp. freshly grated coconut
2 tbsp. chopped fresh cilantro leaves
sea salt and pepper
To serve:
yogurt and cucumber
freshly grated coconut

Coarse semolina is used in this typical south Indian savory breakfast treat. Do not buy the fine semolina used for puddings and sweets, or you will end up with a sticky mess. Coarse semolina is widely available from Indian or Asian stores. This would make a wonderful, spicy Sunday brunch.

one Heat a large heavy-based frying pan over medium heat and dry-fry the semolina, stirring frequently, for 10 minutes, or until it turns golden brown. Set aside.

two Heat the oil in a large nonstick frying pan and, when hot, add the mustard seeds, cumin seeds, dried chili, and curry leaves. Stir-fry for 30 seconds, add the onion and green chili, and stir-fry until the onion has softened.

three Add the raisins, cashews, peas, semolina, and water. Season with salt and pepper and cook over a low heat, stirring constantly, until the semolina has absorbed all the water. Stir in the lemon juice, coconut, and cilantro. Serve hot, with yogurt and cucumber, and freshly grated coconut.

Preparation time 10 minutes Cooking time 18-20 minutes Total time 28-30 minutes Serves 4

mushroom korma

2 tbsp. vegetable oil
1 onion, finely chopped
1 tsp. grated fresh ginger
1 fresh green chili, chopped
1 lb. large button or chestnut mushrooms, halved
1 tsp. chili powder
½ tsp. ground turmeric
2 tsp. ground cumin
1 tbsp. ground coriander
7 oz. canned chopped tomatoes
1 tsp. sugar
3 tbsp. light cream
2 tbsp. chopped fresh cilantro
sea salt and pepper

This is the perfect choice for those who love aromatic rather than fiery dishes.

one Heat the oil in a large saucepan and fry the onions until soft and lightly browned.

two Add the ginger, chili, and mushrooms and sauté for 5 minutes. Add the chili powder, turmeric, cumin, coriander, tomatoes, and sugar. Cover the saucepan and cook gently for about 8–10 minutes.

three Stir in the cream and chopped cilantro, season with salt and pepper, and serve hot.

cabbage bhaji

1 lb. white cabbage, coarsely chopped
½ cup water
1 tbsp. vegetable oil
2 tsp. urad dhal (a lentil)
1 tsp. black mustard seeds
1 dried red chili, finely chopped
6-8 curry leaves
2 tbsp. grated fresh coconut
sea salt

This cabbage dish uses urad dhal, a lentil that has a nutty flavor when it is fried or roasted. It is used widely in many south Indian dishes.

one Place the cabbage in a large saucepan with the water, cover, and cook over a medium heat for 10 minutes, stirring occasionally. Drain, return to the pan, set aside and keep warm.

two Meanwhile, heat the oil in a small nonstick frying pan and when hot, add the urad dhal, mustard seeds, and dried chili. Stir-fry for 1–2 minutes and, when the dhal turns light brown, add the curry leaves and fry, stirring constantly, for 2 minutes.

three Pour this spiced oil over the cabbage, stir in the coconut, season with salt and pepper, and serve hot.

jeera potatoes

2 tbsp. vegetable oil
1 tbsp. fresh ginger, cut into fine slivers
1 tbsp. cumin seeds
1 lb. potatoes, peeled, cut into
1 inch cubes, and boiled
1 fresh green chili, finely sliced
2 tsp. lime juice
sea salt and pepper
fresh cilantro leaves, to garnish

Spiced with cumin, these potatoes go well with chicken and fish dishes.

one Heat the oil in a large frying pan and when hot, add the ginger and cumin. Stir-fry for 2 minutes, add the potatoes and chili, season with salt and pepper, and sauté for 6–8 minutes, or until the potatoes are lightly browned.

two Stir in the lime juice and sprinkle over the cilantro leaves. Serve hot.

Preparation time 5 minutes Cooking time 20 minutes Total time 25 minutes Serves 4

spinach and chickpea sabzi

1 tbsp. vegetable oil
1 tsp cumin seeds
½ tsp. coarsely ground coriander seeds
1 small onion, finely chopped
8 oz. baby spinach
7 oz. canned chopped tomatoes
1 tsp. chili powder
1 tbsp. dhana-jeera (coriander and cumin powder)
1 tsp. amchoor (dried mango powder)
1 tsp. palm sugar (jaggery) or soft brown sugar
1 tbsp. lime juice
13 oz. can chickpeas, rinsed and drained
1 cup water
sea salt and pepper

This quick, tasty dish uses spinach and canned chickpeas, flavored with amchoor (dried mango powder.)

one Heat the oil in a large frying pan and when hot add the cumin and coriander seeds and onion. Stir-fry until the onion is soft and light brown, then add the spinach and tomatoes and stir well.

two Add the chili powder, dhana-jeera, amchoor, palm or brown sugar, and lime juice and stir and cook for 1–2 minutes, then add the chickpeas and water. Season with salt and pepper, cover, and simmer gently for 10 minutes, stirring occasionally. Serve hot.

brinjal and potato curry

1 small onion, chopped
2 tsp. grated fresh ginger
5 garlic cloves, coarsely chopped
2 fresh green chilies, deseeded and chopped
½ cup water
4 tbsp. vegetable oil
1 large eggplant, cut into ½ inch dice
1 lb. potatoes, cut into ½ inch cubes, boiled, and drained
2 tsp. cumin seeds
1 tsp. nigella
1 tsp. ground turmeric
1 tsp. ground coriander
1 tsp. ground cumin
1 tbsp. lemon juice
sea salt and pepper
chopped fresh cilantro, to garnish

Eggplant (brinjal) cooked with potatoes and spices are wonderful stuffed into a sandwich or served with rice and Tarka Dhal (see page 79).

one Place the onion, ginger, garlic, chilies, and water in a food processor or blender and process until smooth. Set aside.

two Heat 2 tbsp. of the oil in a large frying pan and, when hot, stir-fry the eggplant until lightly browned. Remove with a slotted spoon and set aside.

three Heat the remaining oil and, when hot, add the potatoes and cook until lightly browned. Remove with a slotted spoon and set aside.

four Add the cumin and nigella to the pan, stir for 30 seconds, then add the turmeric, ground coriander, ground cumin, and the onion paste. Fry for 2–3 minutes and then return the potatoes and eggplant to the pan. Season with salt and pepper and stir-fry for 3–4 minutes. Remove from the heat, stir in the lemon juice, and serve hot, garnished with chopped cilantro.

Preparation time 10 minutes Cooking time 5–6 minutes Total time 15–16 minutes Serves 4

spiced beets

1 tbsp. vegetable oil
2 garlic cloves, finely chopped
1 tsp. freshly grated ginger
1 tsp. cumin seeds
1 tsp. coriander seeds, coarsely crushed
½ tsp. dried red chili flakes
1¼ lb. cooked and peeled (or canned) beets, cut into wedges
½ cup coconut milk
¼ tsp. ground cardamom seeds
grated rind and juice of 1 lime
handful of fresh chopped cilantro
sea salt and pepper

Gently spiced with cardamom, coriander, cumin, and lime, this dish will change the way you feel about this colorful, but humble root. Canned beets are widely available everywhere; do not use the pickled or packed-in-syrup variety.

one Heat the oil in a large frying pan and when hot, add the garlic, ginger, cumin, coriander seeds, and chili flakes. Stir-fry for 1–2 minutes then add the beets. Fry, stirring gently, for 1 minute and then add the coconut milk, ground cardamom, lime rind and juice, and cook over a medium heat for 2–3 minutes.

two Stir in the chopped cilantro, season with salt and pepper, and serve hot, warm or at room temperature.

Preparation time 10 minutes Cooking time 15 minutes Total time 25 minutes Serves 4

bhindi bhaji

3 tbsp. vegetable oil
1 tsp. mustard seeds
1 tsp. cumin seeds
1 lb. okra, trimmed and cut into
½ inch slices
1 tsp. chili powder
1 tbsp. dhanajeera (coriander and cumin powder)
2 tsp. palm sugar (jaggery) or soft brown sugar
1 tomato, finely chopped
2 tbsp. chopped fresh cilantro
sea salt and pepper
lime wedges, to serve

Okra is cooked in various different ways in India. It can be stuffed with a masala and fried, used in curries, or finely sliced and deep-fried for a crunchy snack. Here it is quickly stir-fried.

one Heat the oil in a large frying pan and, when hot, add the mustard and cumin seeds. As soon as the mustard seeds begin to pop, add the okra and stir-fry for 8–10 minutes.

two Add the chili powder, dhanajeera, sugar, and tomato and cook for another 3–5 minutes. Remove from the heat, season with salt and pepper and stir in the cilantro. Serve hot with lime wedges, to squeeze over.

Preparation time 10 minutes Cooking time 15–20 minutes Total time 25–30 minutes Serves 4

pumpkin curry

1 tbsp. vegetable oil
1 onion, halved and thinly sliced
4 garlic cloves, crushed
1 tsp. ground cumin
2 tsp. ground coriander
1 fresh green chili, finely chopped
6 curry leaves
2 cups coconut milk
1½ lb. pumpkin, cut into 2 inch cubes
sea salt and pepper
2 tbsp. chopped fresh cilantro

Coconut milk perfectly complements the spiced pumpkin.

one Heat the oil in a large saucepan and, when hot, add the onion and stir-fry until soft and lightly browned. Add the garlic, cumin, ground coriander, chili, and curry leaves and stir-fry for another minute.

two Pour in the coconut milk, hot water, and pumpkin, bring to a boil, cover, and simmer gently for 10–15 minutes, or until the pumpkin is tender.

three Season with salt and pepper and stir in the cilantro. Serve hot.

Preparation time 10 minutes Cooking time 8-10 minutes Total time 18-20 minutes Serves 4

mango curry

1 tbsp. vegetable oil
1 tsp. mustard seeds
1 onion, halved and thinly sliced
15–20 curry leaves
½ tsp. dried red chili flakes
1 tsp. grated fresh ginger
1 fresh green chili, deseeded and sliced
1 tsp. ground turmeric
3 ripe mangoes, peeled, pitted and thinly sliced
14 oz. plain yogurt, lightly beaten
sea salt

Use really ripe mangoes to ensure a fresh, fruity flavor.

one Heat the oil in a large saucepan and, when hot, add the mustard seeds, onion, curry leaves, and dried chili flakes. Fry, stirring, for 4–5 minutes, or until the onion is lightly browned.

two Add the ginger and green chili to the onion mixture, stir-fry for 1 minute and add the turmeric. Stir to mix well then remove the saucepan from the heat.

three Add the mangoes and yogurt, stirring constantly, until well mixed. Season with salt, to taste. Return the saucepan to a low heat and cook for 1 minute, stirring constantly. (Do not let it boil or the curry will curdle.) Serve warm.

broccoli sabzi

2 tbsp. vegetable oil
1 tsp. cumin seeds
1 onion, halved and finely sliced
1 fresh red chili, finely sliced
3 garlic cloves, finely chopped
10 oz. broccoli, cut into
bite-sized florets
sea salt and pepper

This delicately spiced dish makes a good accompaniment to a heavily spiced curry.

one Heat the oil in a large nonstick frying pan and, when hot, add the cumin. Stir-fry for 1 minute and then add the onion. Cook over a moderate heat until lightly browned.

two Stir in the chili, garlic, and broccoli. Cover the pan and reduce the heat to low. Cook for 6–8 minutes, until the broccoli is just tender. Season with salt and pepper and serve hot.

shallot curry

2 tbsp. vegetable oil
1 tsp. coarsely ground coriander seeds
1 tsp. cumin seeds
3 plum tomatoes, coarsely chopped
10 shallots, peeled
1 tsp. chili powder
½ tsp. ground turmeric
1 tbsp. dhanajeera powder
1 tsp. sugar
4-6 tbsp. lemon juice
3 large potatoes, cut into matchsticks
½ cup water
2 tbsp. chopped fresh cilantro
sea salt and pepper

The delicate, sweet flavor of shallots is complemented by the aromatic spices in this flavorsome curry.

one Heat the oil in a large frying pan and, when hot, add the coriander and cumin seeds, tomatoes, and shallots. Stir-fry for 2 minutes, then add the chili powder, turmeric, dhanajeera powder, sugar, and lemon juice to taste. Stir to mix well.

two Add the potatoes and water, cover and cook gently for 10–15 minutes, or until the potatoes are tender. Stir in the cilantro, season with salt and pepper, and serve hot.

rice & breads

Delicious, aromatic, and easy to make kitcheree, coconut rice, naan bread, and spiced puris.

Preparation time 5 minutes, plus soaking and standing

Cooking time 15 minutes Total time 20 minutes Serves 4

saffron and cardamom rice

1 tbsp. unsalted butter
1 tbsp. vegetable oil
1 onion, finely chopped
2 dried red chilies
6 cardamom pods, lightly crushed
1 cinnamon stick
1 tsp. cumin seeds
2 bay leaves
1 cup basmati rice, washed and soaked in cold water for 15 minutes
1 tsp. saffron strands, soaked in 1 tbsp. hot milk
2 cups boiling water
sea salt and pepper
crispy fried onions, to garnish

Flavored with the aromatic spices cardamom and saffron, this fragrant rice dish makes a delicious centerpiece for any Indian meal.

one Heat the butter and oil in a large heavy-based saucepan and add the onion. Stir and cook over a moderate heat for 2–3 minutes. Add the dried red chilies, cardamom pods, cinnamon, cumin seeds, and bay leaves.

two Drain the rice, add to the pan, and stir-fry for 2–3 minutes. Add the saffron mixture and boiling water, season with salt and pepper and bring back to the boil. Cover tightly, reduce the heat to low, and simmer gently for 10 minutes. Do not lift the lid, as the steam is required for the cooking process.

three Remove the pan from the heat and let the rice stand, covered and undisturbed, for 8–10 minutes. Fluff up the grains with a fork and serve garnished with crispy fried onions.

Tip: To make crispy fried onions, thinly slice an onion and pan-fry until crisp and golden. Drain on paper towels and serve sprinkled over rice dishes.

Preparation time 5 minutes, plus soaking and standing

Cooking time 15 minutes Total time 20 minutes Serves 4

tomato rice

2 tbsp. butter
1 small onion, halved and thinly sliced
1 garlic clove, crushed
1 tsp. cumin seeds
4–6 black peppercorns
1 clove
1 cinnamon stick
2 oz. frozen peas
7 oz. canned chopped tomatoes
2 tbsp. tomato purée
1 cup basmati rice, washed and soaked in cold water for 15 minutes
2 cups boiling water
2 tbsp. chopped cilantro
sea salt and pepper

This aromatic and delicately flavored and colored rice would make a good dinner party dish.

one Heat the butter in a large heavy-based saucepan and, when melted, add the onion, garlic, cumin, peppercorns, clove, and cinnamon. Stir-fry for 2–3 minutes. Drain the rice.

two Add the peas, tomatoes, tomato purée, and rice and stir-fry for another 2–3 minutes.

three Add the boiling water and coriander leaves, season with salt and pepper, and bring back to a boil. Cover tightly, reduce the heat to low, and simmer gently for 10 minutes. Do not lift the lid, as the steam is required for the cooking process.

four Remove the pan from the heat and let the rice stand, covered and undisturbed, for 8–10 minutes. To serve, fluff up the grains of rice with a fork.

jeera rice

2 tbsp. unsalted butter
2 tsp. cumin seeds
1 clove
2 cardamom pods, lightly crushed
1 cup basmati rice, washed and soaked in cold water for 15 minutes
2 cups boiling water
sea salt and pepper

This simple rice dish, flavored with cumin, makes a great accompaniment to any Indian meal.

one Melt the butter in a large heavy-based saucepan over a medium heat. Add the cumin seeds, clove, and cardamom pods and stir-fry for 30 seconds.

two Drain the rice, add to the pan and stir to coat in the spiced butter for 2–3 minutes. Pour in the boiling water and bring back to a boil. Season with salt and pepper, stir, cover tightly, and simmer over low heat for 10 minutes. Do not lift the lid, as the steam is required for the cooking process.

three Remove the pan from the heat and let the rice stand, covered and undisturbed, for 8–10 minutes. To serve, lightly fluff up the grains with a fork.

kitcheree

1 tbsp. unsalted butter
1 tbsp. vegetable oil
1 onion, halved and thinly sliced
1 cinnamon stick
4–5 cloves
6 black peppercorns
1 tsp. grated fresh ginger
2 fresh green chilies, deseeded and finely chopped
1 tsp. cumin seeds
2 tsp. ground coriander
1 cup dried moong dhal (split yellow lentils), rinsed and drained
1 cup basmati rice, rinsed and soaked in cold water for 15 minutes
2 cups boiling water
sea salt and pepper
To garnish
crispy fried onions and hard-boiled eggs

This traditional dish of rice cooked with lentils inspired the breakfast dish of the Raj—kedgeree.

one Heat the butter and oil in a large heavy-based saucepan and add the onion. Cook until lightly browned and add the cinnamon, cloves, peppercorns, ginger, chilies, cumin seeds, ground coriander, moong dha, and rice. Season with salt and pepper and stir-fry for 3–4 minutes.

two Add the boiling water and bring back to a boil. Cover the pan tightly, reduce the heat to low, and cook for 10 minutes. Do not lift the lid, as the steam is required for the cooking process. Remove the pan from the heat and let stand, covered and undisturbed, for 8–10 minutes.

three To serve, fluff up the grains of rice with a fork and garnish with crispy fried onions and hard-boiled eggs.

Preparation time 5 minutes, plus soaking and standing

Cooking time 15 minutes Total time 20 minutes Serves 4

coconut rice

2 tbsp. vegetable oil
2 tsp. black mustard seeds
1 tsp. cumin seeds
10 curry leaves
1 dried red chili, finely chopped
1 cup basmati rice, washed and soaked in cold water for 15 minutes
½ cup coconut milk
1½ cups boiling water
sea salt and pepper
roasted cashew nuts, to garnish

Lightly spiced and fragrant with coconut milk, this rice dish is the perfect partner for fish or seafood.

one Heat the oil in a large heavy-based saucepan and, when hot, add the mustard seeds, cumin, curry leaves, and dried chili .

two Drain the rice, add to the pan and stir-fry for 1–2 minutes. Add the coconut milk and boiling water, season with salt and pepper, and bring back to a boil. Cover tightly, reduce the heat to low, and simmer gently for 10–12 minutes. Do not lift the lid, as the steam is required for the cooking process.

three Remove the pan from the heat and let stand, covered and undisturbed, for 8–10 minutes. To serve, fluff up the grains of rice with a fork and garnish with roasted cashew nuts.

Preparation time 10 minutes, plus standing

Cooking time 18–20 minutes Total time 28–30 minutes Serves 4

mushroom pulao

2 tbsp. unsalted butter
3–4 garlic cloves, thinly sliced
1 tsp. grated fresh ginger
3 scallions, thinly sliced
½ tsp. ground turmeric
8 oz. chestnut mushrooms, thinly sliced
1 cup easy-cook basmati rice, rinsed and drained
2 tbsp. chopped cilantro
2 cups boiling vegetable stock or water
sea salt and pepper

This dish uses easy-cook basmati rice, combined with mushrooms, scallions, herbs, and spices. The rice needs no soaking.

one Heat the butter in a large heavy-based saucepan and, when melted, add the garlic, ginger, scallions, turmeric, mushrooms, and rice. Stir-fry for 2–3 minutes and then add the chopped cilantro. Season with salt and pepper and pour in the boiling stock or water. Bring back to a boil, cover the pan tightly, reduce the heat to low and simmer for 15 minutes. Do not lift the lid, as the steam is required for the cooking process.

two Remove the pan from the heat and let stand, covered and undisturbed, for 8–10 minutes. To serve, fluff the grains of rice with a fork.

Preparation time 5 minutes, plus standing

Cooking time 15–18 minutes Total time 20–23 minutes Serves 4

spinach and chickpea pulao

1 tbsp. unsalted butter
1 tbsp. vegetable oil
1 onion, finely chopped
1 tsp. cumin seeds
2 tsp. ground coriander
2 garlic cloves, crushed
1 tsp. grated fresh ginger
3½ oz. spinach leaves, finely shredded
13 oz. can chickpeas, rinsed and drained
1 cup easy-cook basmati rice, rinsed and drained
2 tbsp. chopped dill
2 cups boiling vegetable stock
sea salt and pepper

one Heat the butter and oil in a large heavy-based frying pan and, when hot, add the onion. Cook over a moderate heat until lightly browned, then add the cumin seeds, ground coriander, garlic, ginger, spinach, chickpeas, rice, and dill. Stir and season with salt and pepper.

two Pour over the boiling stock and bring back to a boil. Cover the pan tightly, reduce the heat to low and cook gently for 10–12 minutes. Do not lift the lid, as the steam is required for the cooking process.

three Remove the pan from the heat and let the rice stand, covered and undisturbed, for 8–10 minutes. Fluff up the grains with a fork and serve hot.

naan

2 cups. self-rising flour
¼ oz. packet easy-blend dried yeast
1 tsp. sea salt
1 tsp. roasted cumin seeds
2 tbsp. plain yogurt, lightly beaten
1 tbsp. melted butter, plus extra for brushing
4 tbsp. lukewarm milk
cilantro, to garnish

Though readily available in supermarkets and shops, there is nothing like freshly made naan bread. You can also vary the flavorings used when you make your own.

one In a large, warmed mixing bowl, mix together the flour, yeast, salt, cumin seeds, yogurt, and butter. Add the milk and knead to make a soft dough. Cover with a lightly oiled sheet of plastic wrap and let rest for 20–25 minutes in a warm (not hot) place.

two Turn the dough out onto a large board or surface, lightly dusted with flour, and knead for 3–4 minutes, or until smooth. Divide the dough into 8 portions and roll each one up into a ball.

three With a rolling pin, roll each ball out into an oval or triangular shape, the size of a pita bread.

four Brush with melted butter and cook in batches, under a preheated hot broiler, for 2–3 minutes on each side. Serve hot, garnished with coriander leaves.

Tip: Instead of the cumin seeds, you can use 1 tsp. nigellas, poppy seeds, sesame seeds, or 2 finely chopped garlic cloves.

Preparation time 10 minutes, plus resting

Cooking time 10 minutes Total time 20 minutes Makes 10

bhaturas

1½ cups self-rising flour
1 tbsp. oil
1 tbsp. plain yogurt
1 tsp. sea salt
2–3 tbsp. water
oil, for deep-frying

Quick and easy to prepare, these deep-fried puris (puffed bread) are excellent served with Jeera Potatoes (see page 85), Brinjal and Potato Curry (see page 87), or Shrimp with Curry Leaves and Fenugreek (see page 69).

one In a large mixing bowl, combine the flour, oil, yogurt, and salt. Mix well and add enough water to make a soft dough. Cover with a dishtowel and allow to rest for 15 minutes.

two Turn the dough out on to a lightly floured board and knead well for 3–4 minutes, or until smooth. Divide the mixture into 10 portions and roll up each portion into a ball.

three Using a rolling pin, roll each ball into an 3½ inch disk and set aside.

four Heat the oil for deep-frying in a large wok or deep frying pan to 350–375°F, or until a cube of bread browns in 30 seconds. Carefully slide 2–3 bhaturas into the wok. When the bhaturas puff up, turn them over and cook for 1 minute, or until lightly browned on both sides. Carefully remove with a slotted spoon and drain on paper towels. Repeat until all the bhaturas are fried and serve immediately

Preparation time 10 minutes Cooking time 20 minutes Total time 30 minutes Makes 16

spiced puris

2 cups atta or chapatti flour
1 tsp. hot chili powder
1 tsp. cumin seeds
½ tsp. ground turmeric
1 tsp. sea salt
1–2 tbsp. water
oil, for deep-frying

These puris make a quick and tasty snack. They are made with atta or chapatti flour, a medium-grade wheat flour that is sold in Indian and Asian shops.

one Put the flour, chili powder, cumin, turmeric, and salt in a large mixing bowl and add enough water to make a soft, but not sticky dough. Knead until the dough is smooth and elastic.

two Divide the dough into 16 portions and roll each one out to a 3½ inch disk.

three Heat the oil in a large wok or deep frying pan to 350–375°F or until a cube of bread browns in 30 seconds. Fry the puris in batches of 2 or 3. The puris will puff up and, when they do, turn them over until browned and crisp. Remove with a slotted spoon and drain on paper towels. Serve hot or at room temperature. They will keep for up to a week if stored in an airtight container.

desserts

Indian desserts are usually served on special religious and festive occasions. However, these gently flavored and lightly spiced desserts are ideal for everyday cooking and entertaining.

Preparation time 5 minutes, plus chilling (optional) Total time 5 minutes Serves 4

shrikandh

1 lb. curd cheese
4 oz. cream cheese
5 oz. plain yogurt
3 tbsp. sugar
1 tbsp. rosewater
2 tsp. crushed cardamom seeds
1 tsp. saffron strands, soaked in
1 tbsp. hot water
chopped pistachio nuts and rose petals,
to decorate

This dessert, made with curd cheese and flavored with cardamom and saffron, was one of my childhood favorites. It is really scrumptious when eaten with freshly made puris.

one In a large mixing bowl, beat together the cheeses, yogurt, sugar, rosewater, and cardamom, until smooth and glossy.

two Stir in the saffron mixture, mix well, and chill for a couple of hours, if time allows.

three To serve, sprinkle finely chopped pistachios and rose petals on top.

Curd cheese is a soft smooth cheese made from skim milk curds. Cottage cheese may be used as a substitute.

Preparation time 10 minutes Cooking time 10–15 minutes Total time 25-30 minutes Serves 4

banana and cardamom pancakes

4 ripe bananas, mashed
2 cups plus 2 tbsp. self-rising flour
2 tbsp. sugar
2 tbsp. melted butter
½ cup milk
1 egg, lightly beaten
2 tsp. crushed cardamom seeds
sunflower oil
To serve
vanilla ice cream and honey

Bananas and cardamom are an unbeatable combination, so these pancakes are sure to become a family favorite.

one Put the bananas, flour, sugar, butter, milk, and egg in a large mixing bowl and whisk until smooth. Stir in the cardamom seeds.

two Heat a large nonstick frying pan and brush with the oil. Pour in 3–4 tablespoonfuls of batter and let cook for 2–3 minutes. Flip the pancakes over and cook 2 more minutes, or until lightly browned and cooked through. Remove the pancakes with a slotted spoon and keep warm. Repeat with the remaining batter, until all the pancakes are cooked.

three Serve 2-3 pancakes per person, with vanilla ice cream and honey.

Preparation time 10 minutes, plus chilling Total time 10 minutes Serves 4

mango fool

3 ripe mangoes, pitted and chopped
juice and finely grated rind of 1 lime
2 tsp. soft brown sugar
1 cup heavy cream, lightly whipped
diced mango, to decorate

Always try to use the ripest mangoes available.

one Put the mangoes, lime juice and rind, and sugar in a food processor or blender and process until smooth. Transfer to a large mixing bowl, fold in the whipped cream, and mix well.

two Pour the fool into 4 dessert glasses, cover, and chill for 3–4 hours, until ready to serve. Garnish with diced mango.

Preparation time 10 minutes, plus chilling (optional)

Cooking time 18–20 minutes **Total time** 28–30 minutes **Makes** 12-15 squares

coconut barfi

1½ cups sugar
1½ cups boiling water
4 tbsp. butter
2 cups grated fresh coconut
2 tsp. crushed cardamom seeds
1 cup pistachio nuts, roughly chopped, plus
extra to decorate

This delicious coconut fudge, is easy to make and will keep in an airtight container for up to one week, if it hasn't all been eaten by then.

one Place the sugar in a large heavy-based saucepan with the boiling water and bring back to a boil. Cook over a medium heat for 8–10 minutes, or until the syrup is reduced and thick.

two Stir in the butter, coconut, and cardamom seeds and cook for another 10 minutes, stirring constantly. Remove from the heat and stir in the pistachios.

three Pour the mixture into a lightly oiled jelly roll pan (about12 x 8 inches), spread evenly and, when cool, chill for 6 hours, if time allows. To serve, cut the barfi into squares and garnish with extra chopped pistachios.

spiced caramelized pears with ginger cream

1 cup heavy cream, lightly whipped
2 pieces stem ginger in syrup, finely chopped
1 tbsp. syrup from the jar of stem ginger
For the pears:
2 tbsp. butter
4–5 firm dessert pears, peeled, cored, and cut into thick slices
½ cup sugar
¼ tsp. ground cinnamon
a pinch of ground cloves
½ tsp. crushed cardamom seeds
¾ cup chopped walnuts

A sophisticated, but easy dessert that is ideal for a dinner party.

one Make the ginger cream by mixing the cream, stem ginger and ginger syrup together in a bowl. Cover and chill until ready to serve.

two Melt the butter in a large nonstick frying pan and add the pears, sugar, cinnamon, cloves, cardamom seeds, and walnuts and cook over a medium heat for 3–4 minutes, stirring occasionally.

three Increase the heat to high and cook for 6–8 minutes, stirring occasionally, until the pears are lightly caramelized. Serve hot, with tablespoonfuls of the ginger cream.

Preparation time 5 minutes Cooking time 25 minutes Total time 30 minutes Serves 4

gajjar halwa

2½ cups whole milk
10 oz. carrots, roughly grated
1 tbsp. butter
1 tbsp. golden syrup
½ cup sugar
½ cup sultanas or golden raisins
1 tsp. crushed cardamom seeds
To serve:
finely flaked almonds
vanilla ice cream or whipped cream

This rich and luscious dessert, made with carrots, is almost fudge-like in texture. Served warm with ice cream, who could ask for anything more?

one Put the milk, carrots, butter, golden syrup, sugar, sultanas, and cardamom in a large, heavy-based saucepan. Bring to the boil and cook over a moderate heat for 20 minutes, stirring often, until all the liquid has been absorbed and the mixture has thickened.

two Spread the halwa into a shallow dish and let stand until ready to serve.

three Sprinkle the flaked almonds over the halwa and serve with scoops of vanilla ice cream or whipped cream.

Preparation time 5 minutes Cooking time 15 minutes Total time 20 minutes Serves 4

seviyan

2 tbsp. butter
3½ oz. dried vermicelli
1¾ cups milk
1 cup water
pinch of saffron strands
½ cup sugar
½ cup. flaked, toasted almonds
½ tsp. crushed cardamom seeds

This traditional dessert is made with vermicelli. Use the vermicelli found in Asian markets, as it is a finer variety.

one Heat the butter in a large saucepan and, when melted, add the vermicelli, breaking it into smaller pieces. Fry, stirring, until the vermicelli turns light brown.

two Pour the milk and water into the saucepan with the saffron. Mix well and bring to the boil. Continue to boil for 8–10 minutes and then add the sugar. Reduce the heat to medium, cover the pan, and cook until the vermicelli is cooked and most of the liquid has been absorbed.

three Stir in the almonds and cardamom and serve hot or chilled.

Preparation time 15 minutes Cooking time 15 minutes Total time 30 minutes Makes 12

chocolate and banana samosas

2 ripe bananas, coarsely mashed
½ cup dark chocolate chips
12 phyllo pastry sheets, each about
12 x 7 inches
melted butter, for brushing
icing sugar, for dusting

These sweet samosas are delicious hot, straight from the oven. Serve with lightly whipped cream or ice cream.

one Mix the bananas with the chocolate chips and set aside.

two Fold each sheet of phyllo pastry in half lengthways. Place a large spoonful of the banana mixture at one end of the phyllo strip and then fold the corner of the phyllo over the mixture, covering it in a triangular shape. Continue folding the pastry over and over along the length of the strip of pastry to make a neat triangular samosa. Moisten the edge with water to seal and place on a baking baking sheet lined with baking parchment. Repeat with the remaining filling and pastry.

three Brush the samosas with melted butter and bake in a preheated oven, 350°F, for 12–15 minutes, or until lightly golden and crisp. Remove from the oven, dust with icing sugar and serve hot.

Tip: When working with phyllo pastry, always keep the pastry covered with a damp dishtowel to prevent it from drying out, until ready to use.

Preparation time 5 minutes, plus chilling (optional)

Cooking time 25 minutes Total time 30 minutes Serves 4

kheer

1 cup Thai jasmine rice
2½ cups whole milk
3 tbsp. sugar
½ tsp. grated nutmeg
1 tsp. crushed cardamom seeds
½ cup pistachio nuts, chopped, plus
extra to garnish
silver leaf, (varq) to garnish (optional)

This Indian version of rice pudding is delicately flavored with nutmeg, cardamom, and pistachio nuts. I use Thai jasmine rice, which results in a creamier texture. Serve chilled.

one Put the rice, milk, and sugar in a large heavy-based saucepan and bring to the boil. Lower the heat and simmer for 10 minutes. Add the nutmeg, cardamom, and pistachios and continue to cook 10 minutes more, stirring often, until the mixture is thick and creamy.

two Pour into 4 serving bowls, cover and chill for at least 6 hours before serving, if time allows. Garnish with pistachios and silver leaf, if desired.

drinks &
coolers

Tropical and exotic fruits
and spices such as mango,
watermelon, lemon grass,
and cardamom flavor
these delicious hot and
cold beverages.

Preparation time 10 minutes Total time 10 minutes **Serves** 4

mango lassi

3 fresh ripe mangoes, peeled, pitted, and coarsely chopped, or one 8 oz. can of mango pulp
17 oz. yogurt
1 cup water
1–2 tbsp. sugar

one Put the fresh mango in a blender or food processor and blend until smooth. Set aside.

two Blend the yogurt, water, and sugar in a food processor until smooth. Divide the mango pulp between 4 tall glasses and pour over the yogurt mixture. Serve chilled.

Preparation time 10 minutes Total time 10 minutes Serves 4

kesar cooler

1 tbsp. ground almonds
1 teaspoon saffron strands
1 tbsp. chopped pistachio nuts, plus
extra to decorate
½ teaspoon crushed cardamom pods
2 tbsp. sugar
3½ cups cold milk
2–3 scoops vanilla ice cream

A version of this chilled, saffron-flavored milk shake is usually made on festive occasions.

one Put the almonds, saffron, pistachio nuts, cardamom, and sugar in a mortar, add 3 tbsp. hot water and, using a pestle, grind well to make a paste.

two Transfer this paste to a food processor or blender and add the milk and ice cream. Blend well, until smooth.

three Pour into chilled glasses and serve decorated with some chopped pistachio nuts.

Preparation time 10 minutes Total time 10 minutes Serves 4

banana lassi

3 ripe bananas, coarsely chopped
17 oz. plain yogurt
1 cup cold water
1–2 tbsp. sugar
¼ teaspoon ground cardamom seeds

This is an ideal breakfast drink.

one Put all the ingredients in a food processor or blender and blend until smooth. Pour into tall glasses and serve chilled.

Preparation time 10 minutes, plus chilling (optional) Total time 10 minutes Serves 4–6

watermelon cooler

1 large, ripe watermelon
pinch of salt
a few mint leaves to decorate

one Peel and deseed the watermelon and cut into cubes. Place in a food processor or blender (you might have to do this in 2 batches) and blend until fairly smooth. Transfer to a large jug and add a pinch of salt. Stir to mix well and chill, covered, for 3–4 hours before serving.

two Serve in tall glasses with mint leaves, to decorate.

Preparation time 5 minutes Total time 5 minutes Serves 4

mango and mint sherbet

3 ripe mangoes, peeled, pitted, and coarsely chopped
4 tbsp. lemon juice
1 tbsp. sugar
12 mint leaves, finely chopped
3 cups ice cold water
ice cubes

one Put the mango, lemon juice, sugar, and mint leaves in a food processor or blender with the water and blend until smooth. To serve, pour into ice-filled glasses.

Preparation time 10 minutes Cooking time 10 minutes Total time 20 minutes Serves 4

masala chai

6 teaspoons Darjeeling tea leaves
1 cup milk
¼ teaspoon ground ginger
¼ teaspoon crushed cardamom seeds
⅛ teaspoon ground cloves
1 cinnamon stick
1 tbsp. sugar
4 cups water

This milky tea, lightly spiced with ginger, cardamom, cloves, and cinnamon, is drunk all over India.

one Put all the ingredients into a large saucepan and bring to a rolling boil. Reduce the heat to low and simmer for 5–6 minutes. Strain into 4 large mugs or glasses. Serve hot.

Preparation time 10 minutes Total time 10 minutes **Serves** 4

limboo soda

juice of 6 limes
3 tbsp. sugar
10 mint leaves
3½ cups ice-cold soda water
To serve
crushed ice and lime slices

This is one of the most refreshing drinks one can have on a hot summer's day. It also makes a terrific aperitif with a generous shot of vodka.

one In a small bowl, mix the lime juice, sugar, and mint leaves, until the sugar has dissolved.

two Pour this mixture into a large jug or pitcher and add the cold soda water. Stir to mix well and pour into 4 tall glasses filled with crushed ice and lime slices.

Preparation time 5 minutes Cooking time 5–7 minutes Total time 10–12 minutes **Serves** 4

cardamom coffee

3 tbsp. strong freshly ground coffee (South Indian, Colombian or Javan)
1 teaspoon crushed cardamom seeds
1 cup milk
2 tbsp. sugar
2½ cups water

one Place the coffee, cardamom, milk, sugar, and water in a large saucepan and bring to a boil. Simmer for 1–2 minutes then, using a very fine sieve lined with muslin, strain into a jug. Pour into glasses or mugs and serve hot.

Preparation time 5 minutes Cooking time 5–7 minutes Total time 10–12 minutes **Serves** 4

lemon grass tea

3–4 lemon grass stalks, finely chopped
4 teaspoons Indian tea leaves
(Darjeeling orAssam)
3 cups water
To serve:
milk
sugar

one Put the lemon grass and tea leaves in a large saucepan with the water and bring to a boil. Lower the heat and simmer, uncovered, for 2–3 minutes. Strain and serve hot, adding milk and sugar to taste.

index

index